THE NATIVE AMERICAN
HISTORY QUIZ BOOK

THE NATIVE AMERICAN HISTORY QUIZ BOOK

John Malone

Quill
William Morrow
New York

Printed in the United States of America

First Quill Edition

1 2 3 4 5 6 7 8 9 10

BOOK DESIGN BY LISA STOKES

Contents

Chapter One: *The First Americans*

Q. What is termed history, most scholars agree, began only seven thousand years ago, around 5000 B.C., and some would resist going back even that far. But the surface of the earth was populated in many areas long before that, by early Homo sapiens, which had gradually spread out from humankind's beginnings in Africa. How far back are human beings believed to have appeared on the North American continent?

    a. 50,000 B.C.
    b. 30,000 B.C.
    c. 20,000 B.C.

A. The answer, according to some experts, is a. There are others who believe this is too early a date, but most anthropologists are now willing to accept that humans were present by 40,000 B.C.

Q. Where did these first North Americans come from?

A. They came from northeastern Asia, crossing the Bering land bridge that existed between the two continents until about twenty thousand years ago, when the waters of the Bering Strait inundated it. These early Paleosiberians crossed in a series of migrations and gradually spread throughout the North and South American continents.

Q. The spreading North American peoples were migratory hunters, who lived primarily off the big game that flourished then. Of the following animals, which, if any, were *not* present on the North American continent?

   a. mastodons
   b. saber-toothed tigers
   c. woolly mammoths
   d. camels
   e. lions
   f. horses

A. *All were present, and all became extinct in North America following the end of the last ice age. They began to disappear about 9000 B.C., and all were gone by 5000 B.C. It is generally believed that their extinction was caused by a combination of the changing environment and man's overhunting of the dwindling populations.*

Q. What wasteful hunting technique is particularly blamed for the extinction of big game?

The First Americans

A. The driving of large herds over cliffs. The meat of so many dead animals vastly exceeded what could be consumed before it spoiled.

Q. The cultures that developed in North America before 5000 B.C. are divided into periods (often overlapping in different areas) according to the kinds of stone weapon that were used. These periods are the pre-projectile-point stage, the Sandia spearpoint culture, the Clovis spearpoint culture, the Folsom spearpoint culture. How long ago were archaeologists first able to agree upon these various stages?

A. The unearthing of different kinds of spearpoints over the past century led to general, but often disputed, theories about various stages. But it was not until the technique of carbon dating (of the natural radioactive decay of matter) became fully established that real headway was made in the 1950s and 1960s.

Q. The beginnings of agriculture and pottery making in the Americas can be traced back to about 7000 B.C. in Middle America (what we now call Central America). Did it take a long time or a short time for agriculture and pottery making to spread to North America?

A. It took quite a long time. Almost fifteen hundred years passed before the first evidence of cultivated maize (corn) appeared as far north as present-day New Mexico, and it was not until about 2000 B.C. that villages organized around agriculture began to become common in North America.

Q. Only one animal was domesticated by North American peoples. What was it?

A. The dog, beginning around 1500 B.C. The turkey, which might seem a likely candidate, was so plentiful in the areas where it flourished that there was little point to domestication.

Q. Can you name two inventions of North American Native Americans that can be found in use today in snowy climes around the world?

A. The toboggan and the snowshoe. Both were quickly adopted by European trappers and fur traders.

Q. What is peculiar about all the following terms: Irish potatoes, Turkish tobacco, Egyptian cotton, Spanish peanuts, and Hungarian peppers?

The First Americans

A. All these plants were originally indigenous to the Americas and were cultivated and improved by Native Americans.

Q. Did any Native American tribes eat something similar to what we call caviar?

A. Almost certainly. Both salmon and herring eggs were cherished, but the method for collecting and eating herring eggs was particularly ingenious. Fish were so numerous that it was possible to weight down branches beneath the water so that the herring would have something on which to deposit eggs. After the branches were raised, the roe was first dried and then stuffed into animal casings to make a kind of caviar sausage.

Q. What sweet and crunchy snack beloved by children was the creation of northeastern tribes?

A. Crackerjack. Specially bred corn was popped and then doused with heated maple syrup, which acted as a preservative.

Q. How much of the world's current food supply comes from plants that were first domesticated by the Native Americans of North and South America?

a. 24 percent
b. 40 percent
c. 50 percent

A. The answer is c.

Q. By A.D. 500 were the bow and arrow extensively used by Native Americans, just beginning to be used, or not yet developed?

A. The bow and arrow were already in wide use by this time, but the materials used varied considerably in different parts of North America. There were four distinct types of bow, their design considerably influenced by the kinds of wood or bone available in a given area. Most common among the tribes of the East was the self-bow. Constructed from a single piece of wood, cedar, hickory, or white ash, it was the simplest kind of bow, but its very simplicity required extremely deft carving of the wood.

Some Plains Indians used a compound bow made from layers of wood or bone that were glued and lashed together. California tribes often favored a self-bow that was strengthened with sinew, while the bows of Alaska were made from wood that was wrapped with sinew from top to bottom. Some bows, like those of the Seminole, were as tall as a man, but shorter bows were used by the Plains Indians and others who rode horseback.

Q. Which, if any, of the following animals were not used to make bowstrings: deer, buffalo, bear, snake, squirrel?

A. Snakeskin was not used, but the skins, sinews, or entrails of the others were used in various areas.

Q. In 1781, in the manuscript of *Notes on the State of Virginia*, Thomas Jefferson described an archaeological investigation he had made. He made note of a new approach to digging at a site, the first recorded reference to what became known about eighty years later as stratigraphy, which is to this day the most fundamental method of investigation of sites for all archaeologists. What he had done was to make a perpendicular cut down through the site, so that the layers that had been built up would be revealed. What was the kind of archaeological site he had been working at?

A. It was a Native American mound, which was then called a barrow. Such mounds of different kinds and sometimes of very large sizes existed all over the continent, particularly in the Midwest, the Southeast, and the Mississippi Valley. They greatly puzzled the European colonists and explorers since even the Native American tribes of that time could not explain what they were or who had built them.

Q. Not until the 1960s were archaeologists, anthropologists, and historians able to arrive at a consensus about who the Native American Mound Builders were and when they flourished. Did they come to the conclusion that a single or several separate cultures were involved in mound building?

A. *Three distinct groups of Mound Builders have been identified. The first of these cultures, called the Adena after a large farm in Ohio where a large mound exists, flourished in the Ohio Valley from 1000 B.C. to about A.D. 200. The Hopewell culture, which spread eastward out of the Ohio Valley (the mound Jefferson investigated in Virginia was Hopewell), overlapped to some degree with the Adena. It was established by 300 B.C. and lasted until A.D. 700. The third society of this type, known as the Temple Mound Building (or Mississippian) culture, came into being around A.D. 700, and its final vestiges were still functioning during the seventeenth century.*

16

A gathering of three chiefs from British Columbian tribes. They are Tsalhalis, chief of the Pavilion tribe of British Columbia *(third from left in dark coat)* with two from his tribe; Setakanim, chief of the Clayoquot and a celebrated warrior *(fifth from left);* and Wacas, chief of the Komouks (Comox) of Vancouver Island *(far right).* Also present is Quashinism, a Shesaht from the Barclay Sound of Vancouver Island *(in front of tree)* and Aan-a-klyn, a Nittinaht Indian also from Vancouver Island *(front, far left).*

Q. During the tenth century a number of bands broke away from the people known as Athapascan in the present-day U.S. Northwest and migrated southward. What still-important Native American people were these migrating bands the ancestors of?

A. The Navajo. The migrating Athapascan rapidly created their own distinct culture, but toward the end of the thirteenth century a prolonged drought and raids from the northern Athapascan brought about the abandonment of many of the pueblo cities they had built.

Q. It is clear that most Native Americans of North America learned how to make pottery from the Native Americans of Mexico, who had developed the craft much earlier. Is there any evidence that some North American peoples may have discovered the pottery-making process for themselves?

A. Yes. The prehistoric peoples of the area called the Four Corners, where Utah, New Mexico, Arizona, and Colorado share a common border, may well have stumbled on to pottery making on their own. These peoples, whom the later Navajo called the Anasazi ("Ancient Ones"), were fine basket weavers. There are archaeologi-

The First Americans

cal remains indicating that women lined some of these baskets with clay to make them waterproof. Clearly they were used for cooking, with the basket placed near the fire. It is surmised that on occasion one of the baskets would catch fire, which would destroy the basket but leave a harder clay lining. The next step would have been to burn the basket deliberately in order to harden the lining, followed by an understanding that a pot could be fashioned without using a basket. Simple decorations were then added, and by about the year 700 pottery making had become fully established, with great intricacy and color range added to the designs.

Q. Scholars have divided the Native American languages of North and South America into twelve major groupings. Recognizing that there is some spillover within language groups between South American and North American groups, which of the following figures best represents the number of individual languages in North America alone?

a. 145
b. 200
c. 255

A. The answer is b. The differences between these two hundred languages, even those in the same group, are not a matter of dialect or different words for some things. They are utterly distinct, some of them as different as, say, Greek and German. The individual tribes were remarkably resistant to learning one another's languages, and communication difficulties were one of the factors that contributed to the uniqueness of so many Native American cultures. Some neighboring tribes did develop a "second" minimal language to use in communicating with one another, but sign language was the customary mode of exchange.

As the Europeans made deeper and deeper incursions into Native American territories, some Native Americans made a specialty of learning at least some English and more than one tribal language. These men served as translators at councils and peace conferences, but they were often questioned about the accuracy of their translations.

Q. Which of the following figures best represents the number of words in most tribal languages?

   a. 1,500–2,500
   b. 4,000–6,000
   c. 7,000–11,000

A. *The answer is c. Some Native American languages had as many as nineteen thousand words, and the grammar was complex. The English language has a far richer vocabulary (some thirty thousand words were coined by Shakespeare alone, and many others have been adopted from a host of other languages), but few people use more English words than exist in the majority of Native American languages.*

Q. What were Chinook jargon and Mobilian jargon?

A. These were trading "languages" that took words from a variety of Native American languages to produce a hybrid with a small vocabulary that could facilitate the exchange of goods. The Chinook jargon was used in the Northwest; the Mobilian jargon in the Southeast. But most areas used sign language, which was at least as precise and highly developed as the hybrid jargons.

Q. Did most Native Americans have surnames, as in various European languages, including English?

A. No, there were no family names as such, except in cases in which one great chief's name was taken as a ceremonial title by his descendants, as happened with Hiawatha, but even this was not a surname in the European sense. Each Native American had his own individual name. A male would be given a name at birth, but later he was free to change it to something else. In some cases several such changes might be made in the course of a lifetime.

Q. What were "ten handclasps" or "the whole hand hundred"?

A. They were ways of saying "one thousand," used by the Iroquois and the Kiowa respectively. The great majority of Native American peoples used a finger-counting system, with twenty sometimes designated by toe or knuckle counting.

Q. Using shells, pitch, and an acid bath derived from cacti, the Hohokam tribe invented a process as early as A.D. 1000 that Europeans did not develop until nearly five centuries later. What is this decorative process?

A. Etching. A shell was coated with pitch, which would protect it from the acid bath, and then patterns were drawn on it. Wherever the pitch was removed, the acid ate away at the shell, leaving a pattern with a raised surface of protected shell. Makers of armor in Europe figured out how to do the same thing with metal around

The First Americans

1450, and Albrecht Dürer extended and refined the process fifty years later.

Q. Minerals from quartz to soapstone, the bones, horns, and claws of animals, as well as various parts of many plants were used to make what decorative items?

A. Beads. Decorating with beads was almost universal among Native Americans, but the materials used depended to a large extent on what was available in a particular area. There were, however, some peoples—as far back as the Hopewell Mound Builders—who were much more given to trade than others, and their beads might be made from materials that came from as much as a thousand miles away to the west and, less often, the east.

Q. It was around 1050 that the Great Pueblo Period began at Mesa Verde and Chaco Canyon. What was it about these two communities that fostered the development of such crafts as decorated pottery and baskets?

A. Improved agricultural techniques meant that there was not only an ample food supply but a surplus that could be counted on.

Thus it was possible for those who were skilled at crafts to be spared from work in the fields to concentrate on their art. Both these communities were abandoned around 1300, however, apparently because of a long drought. The new communities that were established were smaller and more scattered.

Q. Around A.D. 1150 a group of Pueblo Indians built the town of Oraibi in what is now New Mexico. What unique status does this town hold in American history?

A. *It is the oldest continuously occupied town in the United States.*

Q. Did the adobe bricks of the Pueblo Indians predate the arrival of the Spanish in the Southwest?

A. *No. On the whole, Europeans learned considerably more from the Native Americans than vice versa, but this was one case in which the Spanish showed the Pueblo Indians how to make bricks of uniform size in wooden frames. Adobe had been used for centuries in building dwellings, but in the form of round balls that were the equivalent of stones.*

The First Americans

Q. Among the Pueblo Indians both the Hopi and the Zuñi had matrilineal societies, but the degree to which that was so was particularly pronounced among the Zuñi. Which of the following three reasons is of by far the greatest importance in bringing about the establishment of a matrilineal society?

a. Having no real enemies, and thus no need for a warrior class.
b. Having a settled agricultural society that made use of natural rainfall rather than irrigation.
c. The dictates of religious beliefs.

A. The answer is b. While the absence of enemies certainly played a role, anthropologists have noted that around the world most societies that are matrilineal and matrilocal (meaning that the husband goes to live with his wife's family) practice what is essentially gardening. If large irrigation projects are needed, along with hard male labor for the building of them, a matrilineal society is less likely to develop. Among the Zuñi the matrilineal aspect meant that all produce from agriculture—and even any game hunted by the men—were controlled by the women. A woman's brothers and sons were the important males in the family; a woman could divorce a man simply by putting his belongings outside the house. He in turn would always be welcomed back by his sister.

Shouswap Indians of British Columbia

The First Americans

Q. Among the Hopi there was an individual known as the Sun Watcher. What important role did he play in Hopi life?

A. *He directed the yearly cycle of planting. When the sun rose at a certain fixed point on the horizon, he knew that it was time to plant a given crop.*

Q. Did the Hopi believe in reincarnation?

A. *Yes. They believed that a person was born to the earth. When the individual's earth death occurred, the person was then born to the underworld, where he or she would again eventually die and then be born again to the earth.*

Q. The number of fish that were available to the tribes of the Northwest Coast of present-day America is almost beyond imagining today. During the migration upriver to spawn, salmon filled the waters from one bank to the other as far as the eye could see. Cod and halibut were equally plentiful in the coastal waters, and numerous other varieties of fish and shellfish

could be harvested almost without trying. What was the particular use that the people made of the candlefish?

*A. This fish was too oily to make good eating, but its very
excess of oil made it a perfect candle. All that had to be done was to
thread it with a wick of some kind.*

Q. Although the leaders of Native American tribes across
the continent came to be called chiefs, only in the southeastern
United States and, most notably, in the Northwest were
tribes organized in a way that leads anthropologists to label
them as true chiefdoms. The development of a chiefdom in
this sense depended on an especially abundant environment.
But even that was not enough. What was the special element
in the development of a chiefdom?

*A. The chief's ability to create a surplus by developing tech-
niques for preserving food. The peoples of the Northwest Coast had
a particular genius in this regard. They had learned to preserve even
fish by smoking long before the appearance of Europeans.*

Q. Why have the Native Americans of the North always
disliked the name Eskimo?

The First Americans

A. It was not their name for themselves, being given to them by the Abnaki or the Chippewa; both languages have similar words that mean "eaters of raw flesh." Although the Native Americans of the North have always included raw food in their diets, they have also cooked food, using the oil from whales and other marine life, and feel that Eskimo is a disparaging name. The name Inuit, which is what they call themselves and which simply means "the people," is preferred. Aleut is also acceptable, although the Aleut are essentially a distinctive group of Inuit.

Q. Did the Inuit and Aleut cross over to North America while the Bering land bridge still existed?

A. No, they were relative latecomers, crossing by boat from Russia between 3000 and 1000 B.C. Unlike the earlier migratory groups, they stayed put in the northernmost habitable regions of the continent, creating a remarkably complex culture for such a forbidding environment.

Q. What part did hot water play in the making of a dugout canoe?

A. After a tree trunk had been hollowed out through a long process of burning and chipping with bone or stone tools, the cavity

29

was filled with water, which was then heated by dropping hot stones in it. The hot water softened the sides sufficiently so that crossthwart pieces of wood could be placed inside to bulge the sides outward. A large dugout could carry as many as fifty men.

Q. What was the most common method used by Native Americans for starting a fire?

A. Two sticks of wood were used. One was held stationary, while the other was twirled between the palms against it to produce an ash or coal hot enough to ignite tinder formed by anything from bark to bird feathers. Many tribes were superstitious about the kind of wood used for this highly skilled technique, but in fact, the chosen wood was always common to an area, whether it was the cottonwood of the Southwest, the cedar of the Northwest, or the elm of the Northeast.

Q. What was invented by Native Americans as far back as three thousand years ago that is still commonly used by waterfowl hunters?

A. The duck decoy. Some decoys were fashioned from stuffed animal skins that were decorated with feathers; others were carved from wood and painted.

The First Americans

Q. Name the ancient Native American game, played with a ball and a stick equipped with a net, that was taken up by the English and is still an important sport at many private schools and colleges in the United States.

A. *Lacrosse.*

Q. Did any Native Americans drink alcoholic beverages before the arrival of Europeans?

A. *Yes. Although the use of alcohol was far from universal, it was common in the Southwest, where wine was made from cacti. Wine was also fermented from persimmons in the Southeast.*

Q. How many Native Americans are believed to have inhabited the North American continent at the time of the first European settlements?

    a. three to four million
    b. six to seven million
    c. ten to twelve million

A. The answer is c. These figures have been hotly debated for three centuries. There are still those who insist on a lesser figure, and others who promote a higher one, but a fairly broad consensus has settled on ten to twelve million, on the basis of combined evidence from many different fields.

Chapter Two: *Colonists*

Q. Which of the following explorers was responsible for the idea that Native Americans should be called red men?

 a. Sebastian Cabot
 b. Juan Ponce de León
 c. Jacques Cartier

A. The answer is a. While exploring the Northeast Coast at the start of the sixteenth century, Sebastian Cabot wrote of encountering on Newfoundland a tribe called the Beothuk that he described as "people painted with red ocher." Although the Beothuk in fact had light brown skin color, the term "red man" was picked up and became very popular among Europeans.

Q. In 1512 Pope Julius II issued a decree concerning the native peoples of the Americas. What was it?

A. That they were descended from Adam and Eve. This opened the way, of course, for rigorous attempts by missionaries to awaken Native Americans to their "true religion," Christianity.

A woman of the Fox tribe of Iowa, doing beadwork

Colonists

Q. In 1525 and 1526 two separate Spanish expeditions to the Atlantic coast of North America did what to the Native Americans they encountered?

A. Kidnapped them and took them back to Spain as slaves. More than one hundred men were captured in the second raid.

Q. The French explorer Jacques Cartier noted in 1535 that northeastern Native American tribes boiled the bark and needles of evergreen trees to make a potion that cured a disease that often afflicted both Native Americans and European explorers during the winter months in the north. What was the disease?

A. Scurvy. Two hundred-odd years later a Scottish naval physician named James Lind stumbled on Cartier's account and began experiments to find the cause of scurvy, which also was a serious problem among British seamen on long voyages. He did not learn that the cause was a lack of vitamin C (which was not isolated until 1911), but he did recognize that limes prevented the disease. From then on British ships were provided with a supply of the fruit, which is why their sailors came to be called limeys.

Q. In 1539 the Spanish explorer Estevan the Moor was killed by Zuñi. Was his death brought about by his unfamiliarity with Native American ways?

A. No. Although this was his first contact with the various Pueblo tribes, he had trekked from the Gulf of Mexico to the Gulf of California during the years 1528 to 1536, living among many tribes along the way. A survivor of an ill-fated expedition whose ship was destroyed in 1528, he was probably more knowledgeable about Native Americans than any man of his time.

Q. In 1540, when Hernando de Soto was exploring the Savannah River in what became Georgia, his party was met by a Native American girl, who was the niece of the chieftainess of a Muskogee town called Cofitachiqui. On behalf of her aunt, she gave the explorer a string of pearls. How did De Soto repay this gesture of friendship?

A. He kidnapped the girl to use as a hostage to protect his party. The Lady of Cofitachiqui, as she came to be called, was more than a match for De Soto, however. Not only did she escape two weeks later, but she managed to take away with her a box of pearls that De Soto had confiscated.

Colonists

Q. When the exploring party of Francisco Vásquez de Coronado first saw bison (more commonly, if inaccurately, called buffalo) in the year 1541 in what is now Kansas, the scribe of the expedition took note of the many uses the Native Americans made of the animal: consuming the flesh, making clothes and dwellings from the skins, using sinews as thread, fashioning the bones into tools, and even burning the dung as a substitute for firewood. How common was the hunting of buffalo among the Plains Indians at this time?

A. *Without horses, the hunting of buffalo was a very limited activity. Not until about two centuries later did the Plains Indians acquire sufficient horses to give rise to the brief but celebrated buffalo hunting culture. This makes the comments of Coronado's scribe all the more perspicacious. Once buffalo hunting came to eclipse the former agricultural society and became central to the existence of these peoples in ways that affected everything from religious practices to tribal organization, all it would really have taken to destroy the Plains Indians was the elimination of the animal.*

Q. In 1564 a Huguenot leader (trying to escape the persecution the Protestant sect suffered in officially Catholic France) founded a small colony on the St. Johns River in

Florida. The Huguenots were driven out by the Spanish in less than a year, but one of their number brought back to Europe creations of his that were the first of their kind to be seen in the Old World. What were they?

A. Pictures of Native Americans. Artist Jacques le Moyne was the first to draw pictures that rose above the level of stick figures and gave Europeans their first clear idea of the peoples of the New World.

Q. The first missionary school for Native Americans of North America was founded by Jesuits in 1568. Where was it?

A. Havana, Cuba. The children were brought there by ship from Florida. The endless attempt to Europeanize Native Americans, and later to "Americanize" them, was under way.

Q. What confederation that would have a significant influence on the U.S. Constitution was first formed in 1570?

A. The Iroquois League. Five independent Native American nations—the Cayuga, the Mohawk, the Oneida, the Onondaga,

40

and the Seneca—joined in 1722 by the Tuscarora, came to an agreement in 1570 that while they would remain self-governing in most matters, in those that affected them all they would act together. For instance, there could be no decision to go to war unless all the tribes voted to do so. The remarkable peace that was thus maintained impressed many colonists. In 1754 Benjamin Franklin went so far as to draw up a plan for a confederation of the colonies based on the Iroquois League, but the time was not yet ripe. Ultimately the concept of a federal government made up of sovereign states became a cornerstone of the new nation born out of the American Revolution.

Q. Under the rules of the Iroquois League, who had the right to vote?

A. Everyone. The votes of the children were cast by their mothers!

Q. How long did it take trained runners to convey messages to all the villages of the tribes making up the Iroquois League?

    a. three days
    b. five days
    c. seven days

A. The answer is a. Although the easternmost and westernmost villages were hundreds of miles apart, they were strung out along a relatively straight east-west line, allowing for remarkably rapid communication.

Q. If a woman's husband was killed in battle, Iroquois tradition allowed her to choose a new husband right away. From what group of men did she select this new husband?

A. She chose him from the prisoners taken by her own tribe. The picked man had to prove himself, however, by running a gauntlet to the home of the widow between lines of whip-wielding women and children. If he faltered, he was killed.

Q. Wampum—strings of white shells or belts decorated with the shells—was often used as money among Indians. What other purpose did wampum serve among the Iroquois?

A. It was used to certify the terms of treaties, whether with other tribes or with Europeans. As Wendell H. Oswalt puts it, the terms of the "agreement were 'talked into' the beads, and the Keeper of the Wampum taught the associated texts to his successors."

Colonists

Q. What ceremonial title did Captain John Smith, the leader of the Jamestown Colony, confer upon Wahunsona-cock, the leader of the Powhatan Confederacy?

A. King Powhatan. It may well have been Wahunsonacock's own ambition to extend the boundaries of his confederacy that caused him to tolerate the English.

Q. Did King Powhatan's daughter, Pocahontas, actually save the life of John Smith?

A. This is regarded as more legend than fact since John Smith returned to England in 1609, and the real troubles between the English and the Powhatan did not begin until much later. There is no question, however, that Pocahontas married John Rolfe of the colony in April 1614 and went with him to England, where she was received as a princess. In 1617, after a year in England, she intended to return to America but became ill and died; she is buried at Gravesend in England. Her son, Thomas Rolfe, eventually settled in Virginia, and many prominent Virginians, including John Randolph of Roanoke, one of the most eloquent and most controversial congressional leaders of the first third of the nineteenth century, claimed descent from him.

Q. King Powhatan died in 1618 and was succeeded by his brother, Opechancanough. How much longer did peace survive between the colonists and the Tidewater tribes?

A. Rather remarkably, for four years, but after that there was constant conflict until Opechancanough was captured and shot in 1646. He is supposed to have said as he was dying, in reference to the British governor, "If it had been my fortune to take Sir William Berkeley prisoner, I would not have meanly exposed him as a show to my people."

Q. Sir Walter Raleigh made two attempts to found a colony on the island of Roanoke (named for the tribe that inhabited it) off the coast of North Carolina. The first lasted less than a year during 1585–86, with the survivors returning to England, bringing with them potatoes they had gotten from the Native Americans. The second attempt was at first more successful, beginning in 1586, but when a ship arrived from England in 1590, the colonists had disappeared. There was no evidence of slaughter, and the enclave came to be called the lost colony of Roanoke. Are there any clues to what may have happened to the European settlers?

A. It is possible that they abandoned their colony and went to live with Native Americans. A people of mixed blood, the Croatan,

Colonists

on the mainland of North Carolina, may be their descendants. Following the Civil War the Croatan were officially classified as Free Negroes, but they adamantly refused to send their children to black schools. Eventually, around the turn of the century, they were legally recognized as Croatan Indians.

Q. Two months after the Pilgrims landed at Plymouth in 1620, there appeared in their camp a Native American who had an ability that astonished them. What was it?

A. Samoset, a sagamore (secondary chief) of the Permaquid, spoke English. He had picked it up from fishermen who had been plying the northeastern coast for some years.

Q. Another Native American, a survivor of a plague that had decimated the Pawtuxet Indians, attached himself to the Plymouth Colony and was instrumental in teaching the Europeans how to raise the indigenous foods and where and how to fish, in general helping them survive their first two winters. He spoke far more English than Samoset did as well. How had he learned it?

A. He had been captured in 1616 by Captain Thomas Hunt, who sold him into slavery in Spain. The resourceful Squanto had

An unidentified northern Californian chief with his family. Notice the
Old-World attire, a sign of European influence.

escaped to England and made his way back to the New England coast with fishermen. He died in 1622, another victim of European disease.

Q. It is often related how Peter Minuit, the governor of New Netherland, purchased the island of Manhattan in 1626 from the Canarsee Indians for a mere sixty guilders' worth of trade goods. The point is usually that the tribe was basically cheated, although in fact the equivalent of twenty-four dollars was then worth a great deal more. But there is more to this story. Who really was getting duped?

A. *The Dutch. The Canarsee were in essence the first New Yorkers to pull off the trick of "selling the Brooklyn Bridge." The island was actually held by another tribe, the Manhattan, and the whole deal had to be renegotiated.*

Q. The Dutch had first begun to take control of what is now New York State in 1617, eventually occupying areas from north of Albany to as far south as Delaware and westward to Lake Erie. Focusing on trade, they managed to keep a general peace with the tribes of the region until 1639. After

47

that there was nonstop trouble until 1664, as the increasing numbers of Europeans came into inevitable conflict with numerous tribes. Peter Stuyvesant finally imposed a peace in 1664, but it was beside the point. Why?

A. That year the English captured New Amsterdam, which was renamed New York, and drove the Dutch out of North America.

Q. Following the early days at Plymouth and elsewhere, how well did the Puritans succeed in maintaining friendly relations with the New England tribes?

A. In terms of treatment of Native Americans the Puritans have one of the worst records of any group in the seventeenth century. Their religious fervor and low tolerance for outsiders and differing opinions of any kind made such clashes inevitable. But the humiliation and cruelty the Puritans visited upon their tribal neighbors make abundantly clear the degree to which some kinds of "godliness" can turn into something profoundly at odds with the teaching of Christ. The clergymen Increase and Cotton Mather were vitriolic in their statements about Native Americans.

The attitudes of the Puritans were scathingly summed up by the great nineteenth-century lawyer, politician, and orator Rufus

Colonists

Choate, who declared that the Pilgrims *"first fell on their knees and then on the aborigines."* It is with good reason that many Native Americans look with jaundiced eyes on Thanksgiving.

Q. What did the founder of Rhode Island, Roger Williams, insist settlers in the area do when they acquired lands from Native Americans?

A. *Pay for them. He had caused an uproar in the Massachusetts Bay Colony in 1631, when he charged that the royal charter had illegal provisions allowing the seizure of tribal lands. After founding Rhode Island in 1636, he went on to compile an Algonquian-English dictionary, which was published in London in 1643.*

Q. Among the early colonists, to whom did the word "American" refer?

A. *Derived from the name of the explorer Amerigo Vespucci, the word "American" was used by some colonists to refer to Native Americans. But the word Columbus had used, "Indians," based on his mistaken belief that he had reached the Orient, took over. The*

English settlers, increasingly resentful of home country control, took the word "American" to describe themselves.

Q. The Native Americans of Maine and New Hampshire used a method for fertilizing the soil in which they grew corn that amazed the early settlers. What was it?

A. *They placed one or two dead fish in the earth around each stalk. The fish not only provided nutrients but also, we now understand, replaced essential minerals that would otherwise have become depleted to a degree that would have made the soil less and less suited to raising corn.*

Q. Early settlers in New York came upon a well-traveled route through the wilderness called the Iroquois Trail, running between what are now Albany and Buffalo. What subsequent man-made transportation route followed the Iroquois Trail?

A. *The Erie Canal.*

Q. What were Native Americans hired to carry along the Iroquois Trail, beginning in 1672?

50

Colonists

A. The mail.

Q. Hostilities between Delaware Indians and the Dutch erupted in 1655 and continued for the next nine years. Why were these hostilities called the Peach Wars?

A. Because, as was often the case, the cause of the Indian uprising was a single avoidable incident, in this case the killing of a Delaware Indian woman simply because she picked peaches in a farmer's garden.

Q. In 1641 a Dutch farmer living on Staten Island, between Manhattan and the New Jersey shore, was killed by a group of Raritan Indians from upper New Jersey. What did the Dutch offer a bounty for in retaliation?

A. The scalps and heads of Raritan Indians. There has been enormous debate about whether Native American tribes practiced scalping before the Europeans arrived. It may be that there were some tribes that did, but it is certain that Europeans, especially the Spanish, introduced the idea to many tribes. The fact that the Dutch offered a bounty for scalps this early is strong evidence that the

Europeans were at least as much responsible for the spread of this barbarism as any Native American peoples.

Q. Of all the Native American tribes the French encountered, the one that most fascinated them was the Natchez, as they called them, centered in Mississipi but ranging west into Louisiana and north into Tennessee and Georgia. What was it about the Natchez that the French found so intriguing?

A. *The fact that the chief of the Natchez was called the Great Sun, while King Louis XIV of France (1638–1715) was known as the Sun King. However, the Natchez had a hierarchical society that baffled the French. There was a strict gradation of classes from bottom to top, but it was constantly in flux since members of the higher classes had to marry someone from a lower class. Indeed, the son of the Great Sun was obliged to marry a woman of the very lowest class, called Stinkards, and could not succeed to the chiefdom; it would be several generations before anyone of his line might again be eligible to become a Great Sun. The Natchez were quickly decimated by European diseases as well as by the hostilities between the French and British, and the French killed almost all of them following a 1699 uprising, long before the death of their own Sun King.*

Colonists

Q. The Natchez had unusual furnishings in their homes. What were they?

A. Beds. Constructed from poles and canes, they had bearskin mattresses and covers made from buffalo skins.

Q. How many different dishes with specific names that were made from corn did the Natchez have?
   a. fifteen
   b. forty
   c. sixty

A. The answer is b. This was a very high number of recipes among Native American peoples; it indicates not only the creativity of the Natchez but also the sophistication of their language.

Q. Among the Natchez was it common for young men and women to have sex with various partners before marriage?

A. Yes. Women, however, did not consent to sex unless they were given presents. In a way entirely at odds with European mores, prospective husbands were proud of how much wealth a bride had acquired by granting sexual favors!

Q. What were the kachina dolls of the Pueblo Indians used for?

A. *These representations of more than one hundred spirits, each accorded an individual name and a particular shape and costume, were used to instruct children in the nature of the spirits.*

Q. During Pueblo religious ceremonies the participants donned kachina masks. What part did these masks play in a Spanish raid on the Pueblo in 1661?

A. *The masks were the object of the raids. The Spanish destroyed hundreds of them in an attempt to stamp out the religion.*

Q. In the 1670s Native Americans along the East Coast decorated their clothing with a new kind of material. What was it?

Colonists

A. Glass beads imported from Europe. They quickly spread across the country, displacing the porcupine quills, shells, and other natural materials that had previously been used.

Q. Why did the Cahuilla Indians of California hollow out the tops of logs to about a foot deep, then set them upright in the ground near their dwellings?

A. With the use of another two-foot-long piece of wood, an oversize mortar and pestle was formed, which was used to grind mesquite beans (pods) in. The liquid from the beans was used in cooking, and the finely ground remnants were made into flat dried cakes that could be stored for later eating.

Q. Among the Cahuilla, why were children very often not given names until they were from four to twelve years old?

A. The formal naming ceremony did not take place until there were several young children among the band and the parents of all of them could afford the great feast that was called for. The ceremony was an elaborate one, at which fathers also sometimes took new

Yellow Feather, a Maricopa. Her headpiece was designed to balance on her head while holding whatever she was carrying.

names to emphasize a greater standing. If hard times prevented a child from being named before he or she was thirteen, the nickname by which the child had been called
continued to be used for the rest of that individual's life.

Q. In June 1675 a conflict known as King Philip's War
broke out in the New England colonies. What nationality
was King Philip?

A. *King Philip was the name the colonists had given to an
Algonquian chief whose native name was Metacom. He was the
younger son of Chief Massasoit of the Wampanoag, who had befriended the Puritans who landed at Plymouth. Metacom's elder
brother, Wamsutta (from which a brand name for bed linens is
taken), had succeeded his father but then died. His people believed
that he had been poisoned when he was ordered to report for questioning by colonial officials, but it may have been that he contracted
some disease during those meetings.*

Q. King Philip's War grew out of mounting Native
American grievances against the colonists on issues ranging
from land grabbing to the application of British laws to the

Native Americans. The conflict lasted fourteen months. When it was over, what happened to Metacom's people?

A. His entire tribe, as well as his allies, the Nipmuc and the Narraganset, was almost entirely exterminated. He himself was killed and hacked to pieces, and his wife and son, along with many others, were sold into slavery in the West Indies.

Q. In 1676, after a series of retaliatory incidents on the part of both Native Americans and British settlers in Virginia and Maryland had left several dead on each side, a man named Nathaniel Bacon led a group of vigilantes in attacking several tribes. Why were his activities a great embarrassment to Sir William Berkeley, the seventy-year-old royal governor of Virginia?

A. Bacon was a younger cousin of Berkeley's. He had no use for Native Americans whatsoever and scarcely more for his cousin or for royal authority in general. Bacon managed to extract a commission from the Virginia House of Burgesses, making him commander in chief of the widening war he himself had been instrumental in fomenting. Berkeley nullified the commission and branded his cousin a traitor. Bacon then attacked Jamestown and burned it. What was probably tuberculosis killed Bacon before he could create more havoc,

Colonists

but Berkeley's reputation was destroyed, and he was recalled to England. The greatest losers in this essentially colonial dispute were as always the tribes in the area, a number of whose chiefs had been massacred while carrying a flag of truce and several of whose villages had been burned.

Q. What part did knotted cords play in the Pueblo Rebellion, led by the Tewa medicine man Popé, in August 1680?

A. Popé had these knotted cords distributed to numerous chiefs in New Mexico and Arizona, to indicate the number of days before a general uprising against the Spanish, planned for August 11. To some chiefs who were Christianized and whom he suspected likely to take the Spanish side, he sent cords that indicated the uprising would take place two days later, on August 13. This "disinformation" was relayed to the Spanish, who were thus taken by surprise when the uprising went off as scheduled on the eleventh. The battles in various areas lasted until August 21, with four hundred Spanish dead, including twenty-one friars, and the remaining settlers withdrew to Mexico. They did not return for ten years.

Q. At the time of the 1680 uprising, approximately how long had it been since the Pueblo had tried to resist the Spanish?

a. forty years
b. eighty years
c. one hundred years

A. The last uprising had taken place eighty-two years before, in 1598. It was a small, localized attack on the Spanish, who returned a year later and killed at least eight hundred at Acoma Pueblo. They also mutilated surviving males over twenty-five by cutting off one foot and enslaved hundreds of women and younger males.

Q. In 1730 a Cherokee village chief named Moytoy was crowned emperor of all the Cherokee. Was this a traditional position of leadership?

A. No. Prior to that time each village had been autonomous, with its own leader. The British, seeking more control over the activities of the Cherokee, decided to hold all Cherokee responsible if the inhabitants of one village attacked settlers. The British representative in the Carolinas, Alexander Cuming, conceived the idea of creating an "emperor" in order to promote more centralized— and thus more manageable—government among the Cherokee.

60

Colonists

Q. Which of the following colleges was an early magnet for Native American students?

    a. Harvard (established 1636)
    b. Yale (established 1701)
    c. William and Mary (established 1693)

A. The answer is c, Virginia's College of William and Mary. Subsequently the Connecticut institution Moor's Indian Charity School, which was established in 1759 and moved to New Hampshire to become Dartmouth College in 1769, made a continuing effort to attract Native American students.

Q. The first of the seventy-five-year series of conflicts between the French and English known as the French and Indian Wars, was King William's War, which broke out in 1689. The Iroquois League generally took the side of the British in these conflicts. What major family of tribes largely sided with the French?

A. The Iroquois' old enemies, the Algonquian tribes.

Q. The English colonists in the Carolinas were determined to prevent the Spanish from moving northward out of Florida. In January 1704 they gathered a force of one thousand men and attacked the Apalachee villages and Spanish missions in northern Florida. Were they aided by Native Americans in this raid?

A. Yes, there were large numbers of Creek and Chickasaw in the raiding force, which virtually annihilated the Apalachee tribe. The Creek and Chickasaw had allied themselves with the English because of the lucrative trade between them.

Q. A group called the Four Kings of the New World were received at the court of Queen Anne in London in 1710. Who were they?

A. A chief of the Mohegan and three Mohawk chiefs. What was called Queen Anne's War between the French and the English had been in progress since 1702 and was to continue another three years, until King Louis XIV relinquished Hudson Bay and the surrounding area to the British at the Treaty of Utrecht in 1713. The British had depended (as had the French) on the help of a number of tribes, and this salute to these chiefs was a form of recompense.

Colonists

Q. Between 1711 and 1713 there was an ongoing war in North Carolina between British settlers and the Tuscarora tribe. In the end the tribe was driven out of the area and moved farther to the north. How did it fare after that?

A. It managed to recoup enough to become the sixth member of the Iroquois League in 1722.

Q. When the Native Americans first saw the horses that the Spanish had reintroduced to North America, they did not know what to make of them. What other animal did they in many cases initially associate the horse with?

A. The dog. A Cree told at the end of the eighteenth century of going to see a dead horse sometime around 1730. "He put us in mind of a stag that had lost his horns, and we did not know what name to give him. But as he was a slave to man, like the dog, which carried our things, we named him Big Dog."

Q. As tribes learned how to ride and breed them, horses rapidly became the most valuable commodity on the Great

Plains. Did this lead to a great deal of buying and selling of horses?

A. *There was certainly a brisk market for horses, but some experts estimate that a hundred horses were stolen for every one that was bought. The stealing of horses became a new badge of honor among the Plains Indians, with various degrees of bravery associated with different kinds of horse thievery. The art historian George P. Horse Capture and his son Joseph Horse Capture, who has also gone into the field of Native American art, are proud to bear the name given to George's grandfather.*

Q. The Yamasee of South Carolina, with the help of neighboring tribes, attacked settlers on Good Friday, 1715, killing more than a hundred and forcing many others to take refuge in Charleston. Had there been long-standing antagonism between the Yamasee and the British settlers?

A. *Quite the contrary. The Yamasee had befriended the British settlers from the start, even fighting other tribes with them. But the British repaid this fealty by exploiting the tribe in numerous ways, including forced labor. They also rounded up women and children to be sold as slaves when the Yamasee failed to pay debts that the*

Colonists

British had helped them build up by offering them rum on credit. A force under the royal governor, Charles Craven, counterattacked and by the fall of 1715 had virtually wiped out the entire tribe.

Q. In 1737 the government of Pennsylvania signed a treaty in Philadelphia with a chief of the Delaware Indians, Lappawinze. The treaty ceded to the colony as much land as could be walked in the course of a day westward from Neshaming Creek. What chicanery did the governor of the colony use to subvert the spirit of the Walking Purchase Treaty?

A. In what was becoming an all too common pattern of taking excessive advantage of a treaty, the governor had a road built in the wilderness and then hired a professional runner to traverse it far beyond the distance anyone could have walked through actual wilderness. Very few Native American leaders could grasp the need for inserting what we would call fine print into a treaty in order to prevent this kind of tricky interpretation from being made.

Q. Although they did not know about the Bering land bridge, the Europeans who explored and settled North America had a strong conviction that the Native Americans must have come to the continent from someplace else. A variety of theories cropped up. Which of the following theories did not have its followers during the seventeenth and eighteenth centuries?

    a. Native Americans were the Ten Lost Tribes of Israel.
    b. They were the children of Babel.
    c. They had been led into the wilderness by the devil.
    d. They were the survivors of Atlantis.
    e. They had migrated by ship from Australia.

A. The answer is e. Little attention was paid to Australia until Captain James Cook sailed into Botany Bay in 1770, and by then awareness of the vast size of the Pacific seemed to rule out such a crossing in ancient times. But the other theories were all much discussed and written about. It was the Puritan minister Cotton Mather who characteristically proclaimed that the presence of Native Americans was the work of the devil.

Q. In 1750 a Delaware Indian named Nemacolin and a frontiersman named Thomas Cresap finished cutting a trail between the Potomac River and the Monongahela River in Pennsylvania. It was first known as Nemacolin's Path but in 1755 was renamed Braddock's Road. Why?

Colonists

A. The British general Edward Braddock widened and lengthened the trail, turning it into a road over which he could move troops from the British-held Fort Cumberland in Maryland to the French-held Fort Duquesne at Pittsburgh in the midst of the French and Indian War. This was an early example of something that was to happen again and again: Whenever a Native American trail was renamed a road, it meant that Europeans would soon be trying to drive the Indians out of the area.

Q. For what did the British raise the bounty to forty English pounds in 1755?

A. The scalps of Native Americans from tribes considered enemies of the British.

Q. During the French and Indian War, in 1755, the influential New York trader who had built Fort Johnson in the Mohawk Valley managed to persuade the Mohawk chief Hendrick to join him in fighting the French. William Johnson truly respected the Mohawk and had always dealt with them more than fairly, but there was another, more personal reason that helped persuade Hendrick to join in an alliance. What was it?

A. Hendrick's daughter was one of Johnson's mistresses. The alliance proved a tragedy for Hendrick and his people when he was killed in an ambush by the French near Lake George. Johnson was able to regroup his forces, however, and received a knighthood for his ultimate victory over the French.

Q. Pontiac, a great chief of the Ottawa Indians, born in Ohio of an Ottawa chief and a Chippewa mother in 1712, became an ally of the French against the English, although he appeared to change sides after the British gained the upper hand in 1760. Then, in May 1763, he led a number of tribes from west of Detroit into Pennsylvania to join the French and seize control of the entire Great Lakes region. What daring plan did Pontiac devise for the taking of the fourteen British posts and forts in the area?

A. All the forts were to be attacked on the same day, each by the tribe closest to it. Ten were taken. Pontiac reserved the honor of attacking Detroit, which he had previously held, but the British were apparently warned by an informant, and Pontiac had to settle for a siege. It lasted for five months, but then a treaty was signed between France and Britain. In 1769 the chief was assassinated in Illinois.

Colonists

Q. At the end of 1763, in the aftermath of Pontiac's Rebellion, a group of some seventy-five men from Paxton, in Lancaster County, Pennsylvania, attacked a Conestoga Mission Indian village and murdered several of the inhabitants, then went on to kill the remaining fourteen villagers, who had been given shelter in the Lancaster jailhouse. Had the Conestoga done anything wrong?

A. The Paxton Boys, as they came to be known, charged that one of the Conestoga had stolen a pewter spoon and melted it down, but even that mild offense may have been trumped up. These Christianized Native Americans were extremely peaceful. As much as anything else, the Paxton Boys were angry with the colony's assembly, which was dominated by Quakers, for its generally conciliatory attitude toward Native Americans. Two months later the Paxton Boys marched on Philadelphia to exterminate Native Americans on public assistance there but were headed off by a delegation led by Benjamin Franklin. The price of defusing their anger was to agree that they would in the future receive a bounty on the scalps of any warring Native Americans.

Q. Beginning in 1761, the Aleut rebelled against the Russians, who had turned them into virtual slaves in harvesting

Cherokee Indian chief John Ross in 1862

Colonists

the furs of Alaska. For several years the Aleut caused serious problems, but in 1766 a Russian armada attacked with the express purpose of doing what?

A. Killing enough of the Aleut to bring their population down to a controllable size. With cannon attacks from the sea and follow-up land assaults, the Russians succeeded.

Q. A proclamation by King George III in 1763 tried to prevent settlers from crossing what geographical line into Native American territories?

A. The Appalachian Divide. Native Americans were not to be displaced by colonists without the consent of both the British crown and the tribes involved. The colonists, only thirteen years away from revolution and already rebellious against the crown, paid no attention whatsoever.

Q. This food, which grew in the shallows of lakes in the North-Central states, was a staple of the Algonquian. Today it is regarded as a luxury. The British called it wild oats. What do we call it today?

A. Wild rice. It is one of the few indigenous North American foods that agriculturists have had almost no success with growing in other parts of the world. The limited supply available is still largely gathered by Native Americans in the same areas where they have harvested it for at least a thousand years.

Q. On the verge of declaring independence, the Continental Congress in 1775 named three commissioners to oversee Native American relations in the northern, Middle Atlantic, and southern colonies. Had anything like this been done before?

A. Yes, the British had appointed northern and southern superintendents of Indian affairs in 1756. The expansion to three commissioners reflected the delicate political balancing needed to bring the Thirteen Colonies together into a cohesive whole.

Q. The Quaker settlers of Pennsylvania made considerable effort to befriend Native Americans and to Christianize them. The Quaker dedication to peaceful accommodation and the degree to which they stressed tolerance of others should have made them particularly successful at converting Native Americans. Why didn't that turn out to be the case?

Colonists

A. Because the religions of almost all Native American peoples were profoundly connected to ritual. Since the Quakers were possibly the least ritualistic religious group that settled in North America, the various tribes were utterly uninspired by their forms of worship. By and large the much more ritualistic Catholic missionaries had far more success.

Q. Did the Native Americans of North America have calendars as Europeans understood them?

A. No. This was one of many reasons why the time-obsessed, "getting-and-spending" Europeans tended to split into two camps, one regarding the Native American peoples as deeply wise and the other seeing them as ignorant savages. The second group, slaves to "progress," was naturally much larger, as it has always been, and avidly embraced the concept of manifest destiny (for whites), which meant that the Native Americans must be contained or expunged.

Q. How common was it for Europeans who had been captured, or who for other reasons lived among Native American tribes for some time, to stay with the tribe rather than return to their own culture?

A. It was far more common than is generally realized. Many thousands of whites took up the Native American way of life and turned their backs on so-called civilization. Numerous commentators during the seventeenth and eighteenth centuries noted that there were many Europeans who freely adopted life among the Native Americans, while only a paltry few Native Americans wholeheartedly espoused the ways of the white man before it seemed there was no other path to survival.

Q. The Mohawk chief Thayendanegea, better known as Joseph Brant, was an unusual and highly respected man. As a thirteen-year-old he fought in the engagement in which Chief Hendrick was killed, and William Johnson (soon to be Sir William) had taken him under his wing. Johnson married Joseph's older sister, Molly, and saw to it that Joseph received a superior education, in part at Moor's Indian Charity School, which later became Dartmouth College. In 1776 Brant accompanied Sir William's nephew Colonel Guy Johnson, the superintendent of northern Indian affairs for the British, to England. Which, if any, of the following did not happen to Joseph Brant in England?

a. He had his portrait painted by George Romney, the preeminent British painter of the day.

b. He became friends with the young James Boswell, who became the biographer of Samuel Johnson.

c. He was inducted into the Masons.

d. He met King George III.

A. All these things happened. During the Revolutionary War Joseph Brant fought with the British in numerous engagements and was instrumental in rallying his people to the British cause. After the war he was rewarded by the British with a land grant six miles wide on either side of the Grand River in Ontario, Canada, and retained his commission as British captain at half pay. Later he translated the Book of Common Prayer and Gospel of Mark into Mohawk. He died in 1807, a much revered man.

Q. In 1782 a revolutionary militia, three hundred strong, massacred ninety Delaware Indians at Gnadenhutten in Ohio. What was the offense of these Native Americans?

A. They had done nothing, and Gnadenhutten was in fact a Moravian mission where these Christianized people peacefully lived. Their only offense was that they were Delaware, and other Delaware, along with Shawnee and Seneca, had attacked settlements in western Pennsylvania. It was a classic case of the "guilt by association" that often led to reprisals against the most blameless of Native Americans.

Q. Name the Founding Father who wrote the following about Native American governance: "I am convinced that those societies as among the Indians which live without government enjoy in their general mass an infinitely greater degree of happiness than those who live under European government. Among the former, public opinion is in the place of law, and restrains morals as powerfully as laws ever did anywhere."

A. Thomas Jefferson, who was fascinated by the lack of crime within any given tribal culture.

Chapter Three: *Usurpers*

Q. How did the U.S. Constitution drawn up in 1787 and declared in effect in 1789 affect commerce with Native American tribes?

A. *The federal government was given the sole right to regulate commerce with foreign nations, between the states, and with Native American tribes.*

Q. In 1787 the Continental Congress passed the Northwest Ordinance, which called for Native American rights, the creation of reservations, and protection of Native American lands. What else did it do that undermined these pro–Native American features?

A. *It also set forth procedures for developing what is known as the Old Northwest (the area surrounding the Great Lakes).*

Q. The influx of Europeans into the Old Northwest brought on numerous separate attacks on European settlers, and in 1790 President George Washington sent an expedition to the area to gain control. But General Josiah Harmar and his force of nearly fourteen hundred was routed by a confederacy of tribes, including Shawnee, Delaware, Ottawa, and Ojibwa, led by a brilliant Miami chief named Little Turtle. A second commander with a fresh force, General Arthur St. Clair, fared even worse the following year, losing more than six hundred men. But this great victory for Little Turtle simply brought on a tougher adversary, the famous Revolutionary War hero "Mad Anthony" Wayne. Little Turtle, who realized that General Wayne, with three thousand highly trained men, was a grave threat, wanted to make peace. But his warriors, now overconfident, chose a new leader named Turkey Foot and were eventually overwhelmed at the Battle of Fallen Timbers on August 20, 1794. When a treaty was signed a year later at Fort Greenville, how much land did the Native Americans of the Old Northwest give up?

a. land equivalent to half the state of Ohio
b. land equivalent to the entire state of Ohio
c. land equivalent to more than the state of Ohio

A. The answer is c. What had been called the frontier now quickly became a widely settled area of European dominance.

Usurpers

Q. In 1799 an Iroquois named Handsome Lake founded the Longhouse Religion. What was his purpose?

A. *He was attempting to restate basic Iroquois beliefs in the context of the new social order that existed with the movement toward farming and private property. It is not surprising that such a step was taken among the Iroquois, whose league was the most sophisticated form of government among all Native Americans.*

Q. In 1802 Congress appropriated funds to "civilize and educate" Native Americans. But using the rationale of civilizing them, another law also took away a right. What did this law make illegal?

A. *It outlawed the sale of liquor to Native Americans. This prohibition, often flouted, remained on the books into the 1950s.*

Q. From 1800 forward silverwork became increasingly common among Native Americans. Where did such work first appear?

a. the Northeast
b. the Northwest
c. the Southwest

A. The answer is a. *Although the work of southwestern tribes became the most famous and highly valued, the craft began in the Northeast. This is not entirely surprising. The area was a center of silver craftsmanship among the colonists. Well before his famous ride, Paul Revere had established himself as the foremost silversmith in North America.*

Q. What eventual policy involving the tribes of the eastern United States became almost inevitable with the Louisiana Purchase of 1803?

A. *Since the lands acquired from France, cutting a vast swath from New Orleans to the Canadian border of Wyoming, was occupied by so many Native American tribes, it was—at least to the U.S. government—a logical step to create an "Indian Country" in this huge territory and to remove the eastern tribes to it.*

Q. After a winter spent in Illinois drilling for the rigors of their expedition to explore the Louisiana Purchase, Meriwether Lewis and William Clark, along with a party of twenty-four soldiers and sixteen others who were to travel part of the way, set out from St. Louis, Missouri. Traveling up the Missouri River, the explorers reached what is now Bismarck,

Tribal leaders meet with an army council in Denver in 1864.

North Dakota, in early November. Wintering with the Mandan and Hidatsa Indians, they came to know the person who was to serve as their guide the rest of the way. Name this guide.

A. Sacajawea, who came to be known as the Bird Woman. Originally a French Canadian named Toussaint Charbonneau was to be the expedition's guide. He lived among the Hidatsa tribe with his wife, Sacajawea, who had just given birth, but she wanted to come along so that she could visit her own people among the Shoshone. Carrying her son on her back, she soon proved to be far more knowledgeable than her husband. When the explorers reached the headwaters of the Missouri River in August 1805, Sacajawea succeeded in getting horses from her Shoshone relatives, and on these they crossed the Great Divide. Reaching the Columbia River, they built canoes and descended to the Pacific Ocean, becoming the first Europeans to cross the continent through U.S. territory.

Q. What did the Brulé, Hunkpapa, Miniconjou, Oglala, Sans Arcs, and Two Kettle tribes have in common?

A. They all were constituent tribes of the Teton Nation, which was in turn the most important branch of the Dakota Indians.

Usurpers

The Dakota, who also called themselves Nakota and Lakota, were usually called Sioux (another of their names for themselves) by Europeans. Because Europeans had a very difficult time keeping the relationships of these various tribes straight, they tended to hold the simpleminded and prejudiced view that no Native American could be trusted. Even today experts argue about the classifications of various tribes into larger groupings. Thus one scholar who emphasizes linguistic patterns may place a tribe in a different category from that of another who focuses on cultural traditions. One reason for such problems is that over time many tribes moved far from their places of origin. The Sioux, for example, were originally part of the Algonquian group but migrated westward and changed in many ways in their new locales.

Q. One of the main ways in which tribal warriors, especially among the Plains Indians, had of determining their standing was by counting coup. What did this mean?

A. Coup *is the French word for "landing a blow," and the highest honor a Plains warrior could achieve was to touch a live enemy with a blow, a lance, or a special coup stick. To kill an enemy and then to scalp him were also coups, but not of the same stature as hitting him while he was alive. The various Plains tribes developed elaborate and often distinct rituals surrounding the counting of coups, and there were many differences between tribes concerning lesser forms of counting coup. But while touching a live enemy was the highest honor, lying about one's exploits and claiming a coup that was disputed by others were the ultimate dishonors. The complexities of counting coup have been explored in great detail by numerous scholars since this practice served as a major force for cohesion and discipline among the Plains Indians.*

Q. Among the Fox, when a man killed his wife, a trial was held. The jurors were from the wife's family. One of them stood by with an ax in order to carry out an immediate execution if the death penalty was decided upon. Did the jury have to be unanimous in its verdict for the death penalty to be inflicted?

A. Yes. The jurors sat on a platform in a row. When the man who had killed his wife had concluded his defense, one of the all-male jury at either end would nudge the kinsman next to him with an elbow, a vote for execution. If anyone along the line refused to pass the nudge on, the murderer was not killed. Instead his family was required to present material goods as a form of compensation to the wife's kin.

Usurpers

Q. There were many drawings of Fox men by white artists. What was it about their appearance that particularly fascinated whites?

A. The way they wore their hair. They shaved their heads bald, leaving a round tuft three or four inches across at the crown. From the center of this patch grew a scalp lock that was never cut. It was braided and intertwined with dyed deer hair—usually red— and an eagle feather was attached as well.

Q. One Pawnee community on the central plains had thirty-five hundred inhabitants in 1820. How many earth lodges did these people inhabit?

    a. 800
    b. 300
    c. 180

A. The answer is c. Each lodge was about fifty feet across, circular in form, and inhabited by five families. A section for each family was curtained off with mats, but the central area was communal. The Pawnee would move en masse to the west three times a year to hunt bison, living in tepees that were erected by the women.

Even though they were on the move as much as eight months of the year, they returned at regular intervals to their earth lodge community.

Q. In 1822 a young Pawnee man named Petalesharo was invited to Washington, where he was presented with a silver medal by the girls of Miss White's Seminary. Had he befriended settlers in some way to earn this accolade?

A. No. The Pawnee had a traditional ceremony that involved the sacrifice of a young girl, captured from a rival tribe, to the morning star. Petalesharo, whose father was against the blood sacrifice, rescued a Comanche woman in the middle of the ceremony and helped her escape. Because of his bravery, and because he and his father were highly respected, he was not punished by the Pawnee.

Q. What were sacred bundles?

A. These were cloth bundles containing trophies and objects believed to have magical powers. They were common among the Plains Indians, and their value differed greatly from one individual to another. A great warrior or holy man could use his bundle as a kind of annuity. To look inside a sacred bundle could cost dearly, in terms of horses or other goods. In addition, the bundles of the notable were often used in rituals, and payment was again required.

Q. Was homosexuality tolerated among Indian tribes?

A. Many Native American tribes had a unique way of integrating homosexuals into the social fabric. If the visions a young man had during puberty rites indicated that he was homosexual, he became a bedache. *Among such tribes as the Arapaho and Blackfoot, a* bedache *wore woman's clothing, performed women's tasks, and could join the women's societies. In many cases* bedaches *were looked on with a good deal of awe, and it was common for them to become highly revered medicine men. As in the case of Tiresias of Greek mythology, a* bedache *was viewed as having the insight of both sexes and, far from being an outcast, was sometimes a particularly honored member of society.*

Q. The Shawnee chief known as Tecumseh, who was born in Ohio in 1768, was among the most celebrated of all tribal leaders in American history. Which of the following statements about him is incorrect?

a. He tried to form a confederacy of all the middle western and southern tribes.
b. He persuaded his own people to give up the practice of torturing prisoners.
c. He was both a brilliant orator and a superb military strategist.
d. He championed the right of tribes to sell their land to whites, provided they received a fair price.

A. The incorrect statement is d. In fact, Tecumseh took precisely the opposite view, believing that the land belonged to all Native Americans and not to individual tribes. He traveled widely among the tribes of a vast region from the Great Lakes to the Gulf Coast, preaching his vision of unity and military alliance. He had immense patience, but unfortunately his brother, Tenskwatawa, who had developed his own reputation as a prophet, did not.

Q. On a trumped-up excuse in 1811 William Henry Harrison, the governor of the Indian Territory, marched on a village that had been founded by Tecumseh and his brother. Tecumseh had warned his brother to avoid armed conflict until they were ready, but he was away in the South, and Tenskwatawa attacked Harrison's forces. In the aftermath of

90

Usurpers

the battle, although the Shawnee forces had lost fewer men, Tenskwatawa abandoned his village, which was burned. The name of this village and battle was to form part of one of the most famous political slogans in American history when Harrison ran for and won the presidency in 1840. What was the name of the village?

A. Tippecanoe. Harrison managed to inflate the scope of his victory, and when he ran for President with John Tyler, the famous slogan "Tippecanoe and Tyler too" was born.

Q. Partially as a result of Tippecanoe, Tecumseh sided with the British in the War of 1812, hoping to promote a Native American nation through a British victory. Did the British reward him with any kind of rank?

A. Yes, they made him a brigadier general. He was instrumental in several early successes, but when the British retreated from Native American lands in October 1813, Tecumseh stayed behind with his warriors to defend them. He was killed on October 5. His body was never found, apparently spirited away to prevent it from being mutilated.

One of the most famous of all Native American leaders,
Geronimo, a Chiricahua Apache, in one of his most
recognizable photographs, taken in 1884

Usurpers

Q. On August 20, 1813, Red Eagle led one thousand of his Red Stick (Upper) Creek in an attack on Fort Mims, north of Mobile, on the Alabama River. The attack ended in the killing of nearly four hundred whites, although Red Eagle supposedly tried to stop it. As a result, a force of thirty-five hundred soldiers was called into action under a general and future President, whom the Indians called Sharp Knife. Who was he?

A. Andrew Jackson. A series of skirmishes and battles ensued over the next year. The following summer Jackson demanded twenty-three million acres from the Creek—not only the Red Stick but also the peaceful White Stick, or Lower Creek, who had aided Jackson. The Treaty of Horseshoe Bend prefigured, in its harshness, the implacable anti-Indian stands Jackson later took as President.

Q. Jackson was also deeply involved in the First Seminole War, in 1817 and 1818. The Seminole kept disappearing before Jackson could fully engage them, but he marched westward and captured the Spanish fort at Pensacola. This action, illegal under international law, served a larger purpose. What was it?

A. It gave President John Quincy Adams a fresh opportunity to try to pressure Spain into selling Florida to the United States;

93

negotiations for the sale had been deadlocked for years. Adams insisted that the Spanish either control the Seminole or cede the territory; Spain finally agreed, and by 1822 the first governor of the territory, Jackson himself, was able to impose another harsh treaty that called for the Seminole to retreat to a reservation near Tampa.

Q. In the late 1820s it was estimated that there were about 13,500 Cherokee. How many white men who had married Cherokee women were included in this number?

    a. 40
    b. 110
    c. 150

A. The answer is c. There were also about 75 white women who had married Cherokee men.

Q. When Comcomly, an important chief of the Chinook Indians of the Pacific Northwest who had befriended Lewis and Clark and subsequent explorers, died in 1830, his flattened skull was sent to England, where it was displayed at the Royal Naval Hospital as a medical phenomenon for more than a century before being returned to Oregon. What had caused the flattening of his skull?

A. Pressure on the skull when he was very young. To the Chinook a naturally formed skull was the sign of a slave. Concomly himself had hundreds of slaves, one of whose jobs was to strew the ground in front of their master with animal skins as he walked, so that his feet did not touch the earth.

Q. In what part of the country was the Appaloosa horse most prevalent?

A. This spotted horse, which is one of the most popular in America, was named after the Palouse Valley in southeastern Washington, where it was bred by the Nez Percé. The breed almost disappeared after the Nez Percé defeat in 1877.

Q. Sequoya, the son of a Cherokee mother and a white father named Gist, was honored by having the great redwood of California named after him. His great accomplishment in life, however, had to do with language. What was it?

A. From boyhood Sequoya, who grew up among the Cherokee, showed signs of genius. Crippled in a hunting accident, he put his remarkable mind to work on the creation of a full-scale alphabet of the Cherokee language. There were no North American tribes that had a system of writing, but it was clear to Sequoya that the written languages of the Europeans were as important to their power as their superior weapons.

In 1821 he sought the approval of the chiefs of the Cherokee Nation to adopt the alphabet and the written language that devolved from it. The Cherokee, who had been among the first to agree to integrate their lives into the society of the European, took the new written language to their hearts immediately. They learned with such alacrity—many of them were enrolled in English-language schools—that within six years a newspaper written in both Cherokee and English made its appearance, and large sections of the Bible were translated into the new language.

Q. In 1830, in reaction to a number of violent confrontations between settlers and Sauk Indians, the federal government determined to rid Illinois of all Native Americans over a two-year period. The Sauk chief known as Black Hawk refused to move across the Mississippi as other chiefs did. He believed that an 1804 treaty concluded by William Henry Harrison as governor of Indiana Territory was invalid. That

Usurpers

treaty had ceded a great deal of land, in Illinois, Wisconsin, and Missouri, which was to be vacated as white settlers arrived. Black Hawk also rejected the treaty on technical grounds, including questions about the authority of the chiefs who had signed it to do so, but there was a more profound reason for his insistence that the land could not legitimately be ceded, even though a very modest payment had been made for it. What was this reason?

A. Black Hawk held particularly strong views about land not being a legitimate object of sale and was eloquent on the subject. He later wrote: "My reason teaches me that land cannot be sold. The Great Spirit gave it to his children to live upon. So long as they occupy and cultivate it they have the right to the soil. Nothing can be sold but such things as can be carried away." Seldom has the contrast between the Native American view that land was not a commodity and the European view that it was the foremost of all commodities been more apparent.

Q. Black Hawk was initially forced to back down (there were only three hundred Native Americans under his direct leadership), but unrest among other Native Americans grew, and by 1832 the inevitable hostilities broke out. Can you name the future Presidents who particpated in what came to be called the Black Hawk War?

A. Zachary Taylor, a colonel, and Abraham Lincoln, as a captain. The future president of the Confederacy, Jefferson Davis, then a lieutenant, also served.

Q. The Black Hawk War began in mid-April 1832 and lasted until early August. With what shameful event did the war come to a close?

A. With the killing of about three hundred Native Americans who were attempting to retreat across the Mississippi to the very territory they had been ordered to settle in. Many were shot as they tried to swim the great river. Black Hawk lived until 1838, a very bitter man, but still capable of dictating and having transcribed into English an autobiography that stands as one of the finest of such Native American documents. The battle for control was now over in what had been known as the Old Northwest, but it was just beginning elsewhere.

Q. In 1829, under the Removal Act, an official Indian Territory was created to the west of the Mississippi in part

Usurpers

of the vast Louisiana Purchase. As large as South Carolina, Indian Territory was set aside for Native Americans forced to leave the eastern states, this relocation being the principal objective of the Removal Act. What future state did Indian Territory largely consist of?

A. Oklahoma.

Q. Even as Indian Territory was being created, a Native American woman named named Nancy Shawanahdit died in Newfoundland. What made her death notable?

A. She was the last living member of the Beothuk, a tribe that was first encountered, historians now believe, by Eric the Red and Leif Ericsson at the end of the tenth century.

Q. The main tribes affected by the Removal Act were the Cherokee, the Chickasaw, the Choctaw, the Creek, and the Seminole. What had these tribes come to be called?

A. The Five Civilized Tribes, because they—particularly the Cherokee—had gone further than most in adapting to agricultural life and seeking to adjust to the ways of the European world. It was particularly ironic that they should be subjected to the harsh trek from their ancient homelands into a far less fertile no-man's-land.

Q. Many among the Choctaw and the Creek resisted the Removal Act. How did government agents get around this problem?

A. *They bribed enough lesser chiefs to sign removal treaties so that those who resisted were thoroughly undermined.*

Q. The Choctaw and Creek suffered terribly on the long journey to Indian Territory, marched westward by soldiers in groups of five hundred to a thousand. How many died as the result of food shortages, exhaustion, or disease?

A. *At least a quarter of those who set out died before they arrived in Indian Territory. It was all too apt that the route westward came to be known as the Trail of Tears.*

Q. The head Cherokee chief, who had taken the name John Ross, resisted the Removal Act in the courts. The suit went all the way to the Supreme Court. What decision did the Court come to?

A. In a decision written by Chief Justice John Marshall, the Cherokee won the right to stay where they were in the Carolinas. But President Jackson ignored the ruling completely, reputedly saying, "Marshall has made his decision, now let him enforce it." As a frontiersman and former Indian fighter Jackson (whom the Indians called Sharp Knife) had greater contempt for Native Americans than perhaps did any other President.

Q. The Cherokee removal, beginning in 1838, was the most dreadful of all the five tribes experienced. Soldiers often would not even allow them to carry out what civilized ritual?

A. The burial of their dead. And there were at least four thousand who died.

Q. What did Jackson expect to be the cost of implementing the Removal Act?

a. $500,000
b. $1 million
c. $2 million

Unlike many Native Americans who donned grim poses for their portraits, Turning Eagle, a lower Brute Sioux, allows the camera to capture his impassioned personality.

Usurpers

A. The answer is a. In fact, the costs were staggering. The Seminole, who most fiercely resisted removal, engaged in war with federal forces for seven long years, from 1835 to 1842. The Seminole War, fought in Florida, as well as in southern Georgia and Alabama, alone cost twenty million dollars and the loss of a white soldier's life for every two Seminole ultimately removed to Indian Territory.

Q. Although the great majority of the Cherokee were forced to transplant themselves to Oklahoma, some managed to hide out in the mountains of western North Carolina. How many were they?

a. 700
b. 1,000
c. 1,500

A. The answer is b.

Q. A white trader named William H. Thomas, who had lived in the area for twenty years, did a great deal to help the Eastern Cherokee, as they came to be called. Although the Cherokee had to stay in hiding until 1842, Thomas finally managed to get their legal right to remain in the area recognized. He then became their official agent. Why was it that when he ran into legal and financial problems of his own, his creditors claimed that the land the Cherokee lived on could be seized to pay off Thomas's debts?

A. Because the land was, of necessity, in his name; the Indians were not allowed to own land. He had bought parcels for them with the money they had received in payment for their former holdings. It took the intervention of Congress to keep these parcels in Cherokee hands, with the matter not finally cleared up until 1874.

Q. For what particular purpose were the famous Texas Rangers organized in 1835?

A. Their job was to control and subdue the Comanche, who had been presenting problems to both American settlers and Mexicans for nearly fifty years. Warriors to the hilt, and possibly the greatest horsemen on the continent, the Comanche outmaneuvered the Texas Rangers well into the 1840s, and the contest between them continued for decades.

Q. Which of the following bows could shoot an arrow the longest distance?

Usurpers

a. Blackfoot
b. Osage
c. Cheyenne
d. Apache

A. The answer is c. A series of tests carried out at the University of California showed that a Cheyenne arrow could travel a distance of 165 yards. The Blackfoot was next at 145 yards, with the Apache at 120 and the Osage at 92 yards on the average.

Q. Many tribes, particularly those of the Plains, cut grooves in the shafts of their arrows. Was this done only because it aided the flight of the arrow?

A. No. The grooves were intended to prevent warping and to enhance the straightness with which the arrow flew. But there was also a secondary purpose. Once the shaft had become lodged in the flesh of an animal (or human), the grooves served to increase the flow of blood, not only weakening the victim but also creating a trail of blood on the ground.

Q. What did the European call the calumet, and why was it a misnomer?

A. The calumet was called the peace pipe by Europeans because it was smoked at councils in which peace treaties were signed. In fact, it was also a war pipe, a sacred object for tribes from the East Coast westward to the Rockies.

Q. The term "okay" was derived from a Native American word. True or false?

A. This is true. The Choctaw word okey, *meaning "yes, it is," was used in tribal councils to indicate that agreement had been reached.*

Q. The Arapaho, originally from northern Minnesota, moved out onto the plains and became closely associated with the Cheyenne. Did the cultures of these peoples merge in the process?

A. The Arapaho and the Cheyenne shared many customs, and they intermarried, but the Arapaho remained culturally distinct in many ways. They did not learn the Cheyenne language and communicated by sign language. Their burial rites were very different, despite the fact that both practiced the annual Sun Dance. One way

Usurpers

in which the Arapaho were set apart from not only the Cheyenne but also most other tribes was in their beadwork. Instead of being merely decorative, their beadwork told particular and sometimes quite complex stories.

Q. Within a tribe, was there any difference between a clan and a band?

A. Yes. Many tribes were divided into clans, based upon a common ancestry. If part of a clan decided to follow a different leader, the smaller groups were called bands.

Q. What special relationship to Native Americans marked the career of George Catlin (1796–1872)?

A. Trained as a lawyer, Catlin turned to his first love, painting, and became the premier white artist to record the life of Native Americans. He lived with many different tribes during the 1830s. His Manners, Customs, and Conditions of the North American Indian, *published in 1841 and containing more than three hundred engravings and notes on tribal life, as well as many subsequent paintings, is the best pictorial record of Native Americans and their culture created by a white man. There are those, however, who think that Catlin's work was too romanticized, while others believe that Native Americans who watched him work among them began to turn away from their customary art and attempted themselves a more naturalistic way of painting that was destructive to the genuineness of their work. Nevertheless, his work remains fascinating; much of it can be seen in the Catlin Gallery of the National Museum in Washington, D.C.*

Q. Which of the following diseases brought from Europe by whites, to which Native Americans had no natural defenses, was the most deadly and widespread killer?

a. typhoid
b. scarlet fever
c. influenza
d. smallpox
e. cholera

A. The answer is d. Smallpox epidemics occurred across the continent from as early as 1615 in Virginia to California in the 1830s. There were even later outbreaks on the plains. The several epidemics in the West and on the plains during the middle of the nineteenth century could have been avoided, for a vaccine had been available since the start of the century, but there were few doctors willing to venture into these turbulent areas, and even when they did, the tribes often would refuse to be inoculated. There were even occasions when the whites used an early form of "germ warfare," deliberately giving Native Americans blankets contaminated with smallpox.

Q. What recreational vehicle is named after a tribe that lived in the area around what is now Green Bay, Wisconsin?

A. This tribe of the Sioux family was called the Winnebago. The public relations wizards who chose this name for the famous camper might have thought twice about it if they had been aware that in the Sauk language the name means "people of the filthy water," leading the British sometimes to refer to them as Stinkards even though the tribe fought alongside the British in both the Revolutionary War and the War of 1812.

Q. Was the canvas-covered Conestoga wagon used by so many settlers migrating to the West named for its inventor, the place where it was first built, or an Indian chief?

A. It was named after Conestoga, Pennsylvania, a village in Lancaster County where it was first built.

Q. In the Gulf states, to what kind of person did the word "mustee" refer?

A. The word was derived from the Spanish mestizo, *meaning "mixture," and referred to persons who were of mixed Native American and white blood. A more common and more derogatory term that was used throughout the West was "half-breed." Marriages between white men and Native American women took place right from the start; the royal treatment given to John Rolfe's wife, Pocahontas, in England in 1616, however, was replaced by a growing prejudice against such marriages in later years. Attitudes depended greatly on the situation that existed, whether peaceful or not, in differing parts of the country. In some areas the children and grandchildren of such unions, especially the men, rose to considerable prominence and respect. But during the nineteenth century, as the tribes of the plains and the West struggled to hold on to their lands, often responding to broken promises with uprisings, the "half-breed" often came to be viewed in a suspicious and even despised way.*

Q. In 1847 the Presbyterian mission at Waiilaptu on the upper Columbia River in the Oregon country was attacked by the Cayuse Indians who lived in the area. What had happened to Cayuse children who went to school at the mission to cause this uprising?

Usurpers

A. They had come down with measles and were spreading it among the tribe. To tribespeople with no antibodies, measles was a killer disease. The leader of the mission, Marcus Whitman, was killed, and some fifty hostages, including his wife, were taken. Military retaliation stirred up further trouble, and the troops withdrew, but the once-peaceful area became a trouble spot that erupted several times over the next thirty years.

Q. The discovery of gold in California in 1848 proved a disaster to such tribes as the Miwok and Yokuts of the San Joaquin Valley and the gold-rich foothills surrounding it. By how much had this population been reduced by the mid-1850s?

A. By at least two thirds. Disease took its toll, many Native Americans were shot on sight, and their ancient hunting and gathering patterns were totally undermined. The fact that these were very peaceful people left them utterly at a loss in trying to cope with the enormous influx of greed-crazed whites. Unused to fighting, they fared very badly in the Mariposa War of 1850–51.

Q. In 1849 a change was made in the administration of the Bureau of Indian Affairs. It was shifted out of the War Department and put under the jurisdiction of what entity?

A Sioux warrior who was shot in the eye

Usurpers

A. The Department of the Interior. At this point Washington believed that the situation concerning Native Americans was essentially under control. But there would be uprisings for another forty years.

Q. In 1851 at Fort Laramie, Wyoming, a large gathering of tribes, including Cheyenne, Arapaho, Sioux, and others, signed a treaty that gave the U.S. government the right to build roads and establish forts in their territories. Did the tribes actually cede these lands to the government?

A. No, the treaty simply allowed the lands to be used, and the tribes retained the right to hunt, fish, and travel freely throughout the area. But roads and more roads, and increasing numbers of forts within shorter distances of one another, meant that within ten years the government had "driven a hole through the Indian country," as Dee Brown puts it.

Q. Seathl was a chief of one of the tribes in the Puget Sound area of what became the state of Washington. He got along well with whites and was the first chief of the allied tribes of the area to sign the treaty providing that the Native Americans would live on a reservation. In gratitude, the whites in the largest community decided to name their small city after him but spelled it Seattle. He was honored but insisted that he be paid a small tribute each year by the city for the use of his name. Why?

A. Like many Native Americans across the continent, Seathl believed that to mention the name of an Indian after his death would cause his spirit to be troubled. The payments were thus a way to recompense him in life for the anticipated disturbance his spirit would undergo in the afterlife.

Q. During the years 1853–56, fifty-two treaties were signed with Indian tribes, which ceded 174 million acres of land to the government. How many of these treaties were fully honored in the years to come?

A. None.

Q. The name of the title character of Henry Wadsworth Longfellow's famous poem *Hiawatha* was the name of the chief who founded the Iroquois League, and it became a hereditary title for chiefs among the Mohawk of the Tortoise

114

Clan. Did Longfellow's 1855 poem celebrate the actual Iroquois leader or his descendants?

A. No. Longfellow drew on the writings of Henry R. Schoolcraft, who lived among Chippewa in the area of Lake Superior and Lake Huron and across Minnesota and married a Chippewa woman. To confuse matters further, the Chippewa were originally known as the Ojibwa, which they prefer to be called today.

Q. Was the name Apache given this tribe by whites or by other Native American tribes?

A. The Zuñi of Arizona called them Apachu, which meant "enemy," and it was taken up by many other tribes to designate this tribe of raiders. The name was anglicized to Apache by whites, however.

Q. The tall totem poles of the Northwest Coast tribes of North America fascinate visitors to that area. Which of the three following statements about them is false?

a. They should not really be called totems at all.
b. Many of them are nearly a thousand years old.
c. One of their purposes was ridicule of others.

A. The false statement is b. Peter Farb offers a detailed discussion of totem poles in Man's Rise to Civilization. *A true totem is an animal symbol that a family associates with its own particular descent. The word comes from the Ojibwa and means "he is my relative." Farb argues that totem poles may be compared with Texas cattle brands. In addition, one of the unique aspects of the totem pole is that the carvings often serve to ridicule a rival who has been bested in one way or another. And while the concept of the totem pole existed more than a thousand years ago among these people, it was not possible to carve poles of anything like this size and complexity until the introduction of iron tools by Europeans.*

Q. The two most famous Apache leaders in the years before the Civil War were Mangas Colorado, chief of the Mimbreño Apache, and Cochise, chief of the Chiricahua Apache. What was the relationship between them?

A. Mangas Colorado was Cochise's father-in-law.

Q. Did Mangas Colorado and Cochise cause many problems for white settlers and travelers in Arizona and New Mexico at this time?

Usurpers

A. Very little. They preferred to conduct their fierce raids against their longtime antagonists in Mexico and indeed prevented expansion northward from Mexico that might well have altered the future shape of the United States.

Q. In February 1861 an Army lieutenant named George Bascom requested a meeting with Cochise. Did this turn out to be a significant encounter?

A. Yes. What came to be known as the Bascom Affair set in motion three decades of troubles with the Apache. A rancher had accused Cochise of kidnapping his children and stealing his cattle. It was certainly not Cochise's doing, and at the meeting with Bascom, the chief suggested it might have been a Coyotero Apache and even offered to help recover the rancher's children. Unpersuaded, Bascom declared Cochise under arrest. The chief slashed his way out of the tent with a knife, but the rest of his party, including a younger brother and two nephews, were unable to escape. Cochise and Mangas Colorado began attacking stagecoaches and taking hostages, whom they eventually killed when attempts at an exchange failed. Bascom then hanged Cochise's brother and several other Apache he had captured.

Q. Two years later the Army once again proved treacherous. Mangas Colorado was invited to a parley and was immediately taken prisoner. The new commander in the region, General Joseph West, wanted Mangas Colorado dead. What was done to him to give the appearance that he was killed while trying to escape?

A. *As the chief slept, soldiers heated bayonets in a fire and applied them to the soles of his feet. When he leaped up, he was immediately shot.*

Q. When the Civil War broke out, what step did the Confederacy take to deal with Native American tribes?

A. *It established its own Bureau of Indian Affairs. The Confederate government also tried to gain the support of tribes, or at least keep them neutral, by making promises to return lands to them after the war.*

Q. Did the coming of the Civil War in 1861 find the Five Civilized Tribes of Indian Territory, now settled there for more than twenty years, remaining neutral or taking sides in the conflict?

A. *As was the case in most of the border states, Indian Territory was terribly split by the Civil War. The majority of those in all*

Usurpers

five tribes sided with the Confederacy (their roots were in the South after all), but strong minorities supported the North. As a result, there was a secondary Civil War in Indian Territory. Among the Cherokee, for instance, John Ross was still the head chief, and he believed that it was wisest to remain neutral. But one of his rivals, Chief Stand Waite, organized a pro-Confederate Native American force. A minority then supported the Union and were attacked and scattered. Stand Waite earned a commission as a brigadier general (the highest rank achieved by a Native American on either side), and he was the last Confederate general to surrender, nearly two months after the war ended at Appomattox. But the Five Civilized Tribes were now seen as a double enemy in the North: Native Americans and traitors.

Q. The most infamous of all the massacres of Native Americans by whites took place at Sand Creek, near Fort Lyon, Colorado, in 1864. It was instigated and led by Colonel John M. Chivington of the Colorado Volunteers, a military force assembled by the governor of the territory, John Evans, for the particular purpose of fighting Native Americans. What was Colonel Chivington's nonmilitary profession?

A. He was a Methodist minister. His hatred of Native Americans was implacable. Shortly before the massacre at Sand

Creek he had made a speech in Denver in which he called for the scalping even of Native American infants, saying, "Nits make lice."

Q. Why were the Cheyenne people settled in for the winter at Sand Creek so unprepared for the attack against them on November 29, 1864?

A. Because only weeks earlier, at a peace parley in Denver, the Cheyenne chief Black Kettle and the famous seventy-year-old warrior chief White Antelope had been told to spend the winter at Sand Creek and had subsequently been given the go-ahead to hunt bison until regular government supplies could be arranged. They were further disarmed because they had come to trust the U.S. Army commander at Fort Lyon, Major Edward W. Wynkoop. But between the Denver peace parley and the massacre itself, Wynkoop was replaced by Major Scott J. Anthony, who was in league with Chivington but pretended to be cut from the same cloth as Wynkoop. Black Kettle and his people thought they were safe at Sand Creek.

Q. Once the attack against the Cheyenne began at dawn on November 29, what did Black Kettle do?

Usurpers

A. He stood in front of his tent with an American flag raised in the air, having been told that that would always bring the threat of hostilities to a halt. There was also a white flag raised, as later testified to by Army officers who had joined in the attack only to avoid court-martial. At least three hundred Cheyenne, as well as Arapaho who had joined up with Black Kettle, were murdered, more than two thirds of them women and children. Atrocities, including the disemboweling of a woman in the late stages of pregnancy, were rampant.

Q. Was Black Kettle able to escape the massacre?

A. Yes, with a last-minute dash up a ravine. But White Antelope stood where he was, his arms folded, and was cut down mercilessly. He lived just long enough to sing a brief death song, which has become famous: "Nothing lives long, except the earth and the mountains."

Q. Did the massacre at Sand Creek, which was celebrated as a great victory in Colorado, serve to frighten the Plains Indians into submission?

A. No, it had exactly the opposite effect—as was usually the case—and the plains were in tumult for the next several years. What

Chivington had really done was to kill or undermine the authority of the very chiefs who were most in favor of peace.

Q. Colonel Christopher "Kit" Carson had usually had very good relations with Native Americans, often living among them during his career as trader and Indian agent. When he was commanded by General James Carleton, called Star Chief by the Native Americans, to force the Navajo from their ancestral lands to the Bosque Redondo reservation three hundred miles to the east on an arid stretch of the Pecos river valley in 1863, did Carson readily comply?

A. *Yes, although in 1861 he had resigned rather than fight Native Americans. But he was always too easily awed by men of power, and General Carleton persuaded him to take up his commission again. Carson instituted a scorched-earth policy that succeeded in so disrupting the Navajo way of life that by 1864 in what came to be called the Long Walk, nearly eight thousand Navajo had been force-marched to Bosque Redondo. Four years later the Navajo persuaded Washington to relent, and they were allowed to return to their homeland—one of the few relatively happy outcomes in the long history of displacement of Native Americans.*

Usurpers

Q. When General Robert E. Lee surrendered to General Ulysses S. Grant at Appomattox, he shook hands with General Ely Samuel Parker, Grant's military secretary, who had drafted the peace terms. Lee said to Parker, "I am glad to see one real American here." Why?

A. Parker was a Seneca. He replied to Lee, "We are all Americans."

View of the run into Cherokee Strip, September 16, 1893

Chapter Four: *Something Else Died There*

Q. The final twenty-five years of Native American resistance to the usurpation of their lands by whites, from 1865 to 1890, brought to the fore some of the most famous of all tribal chiefs. Can you connect the following chiefs in the left-hand column with the tribes they led in the right-hand column?

a. Sitting Bull	1. Apache
b. Captain Jack (Kintpuash)	2. Oglala Sioux
c. Geronimo	3. Nez Percé
d. Joseph	4. Hunkpapa Sioux
e. Dull Knife	5. Modoc
f. Red Cloud	6. Cheyenne

A. *a, 4; b, 5; c, 1; d, 3; e, 6; f, 2*

Q. Which of the six chiefs in the previous question was the only one to force the federal government to withdraw from Native American lands?

A. Red Cloud. The Sioux were disturbed by the always in-creasing white traffic across lands supposedly theirs alone by treaty. Red Cloud and others were particularly upset about a new trail, established by John Bozeman, that cut through the heart of buffalo-hunting country along the North Platte River. Raids were made against whites, both civilian and military, as they traveled through the region. Some chiefs signed a treaty of nonaggression in 1866, but Red Cloud refused.

Q. Colonel Henry B. Carrington arrived to build new forts in the Powder River country to protect the Bozeman Trail, but the soldiers were continually harassed by the Sioux, Cheyenne, and Arapaho. Red Cloud became convinced that if a detachment could be lured out of Fort Phil Kearny and led into a trap, a sufficient number of warriors, even armed mostly with bows and arrows, could kill all of them. Who was the famous Oglala Sioux, just barely out of his teens, who was entrusted with the task of luring the soldiers into the trap being set by Red Cloud and his Cheyenne and Arapaho cohorts?

A. Crazy Horse, who had become adept at taunting groups of soldiers into following him into such traps. On December 21 the

Something Else Died There

plan was put into action. Crazy Horse and nine others succeeded in getting Colonel Carrington to dispatch eighty-nine soldiers under the command of Captain William J. Fetterman to pursue the ten Sioux. They were enticed into an ambush by fifteen hundred Native Americans, who slaughtered them to the last man. The soldiers were also mutilated—a payback for what had been done to the Native Americans at Sand Creek two years earlier.

Q. The Fetterman Massacre alarmed the federal government to a high degree and caused even some of the most aggressive military leaders to begin questioning the value of controlling the Powder River country. Red Cloud kept up the pressure for another year and a half, spurning peace overtures even from General William T. Sherman himself. What did Red Cloud insist had to happen before he would sign a treaty?

A. Washington had to abandon its forts in the Powder River country. For once the government backtracked and began withdrawing troops from Fort C. F. Smith on July 29. A little more than a month later Fort Phil Kearny and finally Fort Reno were also abandoned. In November Red Cloud finally deigned to sign a treaty. For once Native American tribes had succeeded in driving the whites from their ancestral lands—at least for a while.

Q. In the late 1860s the commissioner of Indian affairs estimated how much it cost to kill a single Native American in the wars that continued to break out. What was the figure?

   a. about $1,000
   b. about $100,000
   c. about $1 million

A. The answer is c.

Q. Was there a particular reason why the Oglala Sioux chief Crazy Horse was given his name?

A. Supposedly a wild horse galloped by at his birth, but there is considerable evidence that white men distorted his real name by calling him Crazy Horse. The correct translation probably should have been "His-Horse-Is-Crazy." English-speaking whites in particular resisted this kind of complex name that was so natural to Native Americans. The tendency to tidy things up and make them more linear no doubt has caused us to lose the true significance of many Native American names. Happily, many contemporary Native Americans insist upon using the full form of their heritage. An example is Marjorie Bear Don't Walk, one of the fifty-three "ordinary" Americans who were invited to the inauguration of President Bill Clinton.

Something Else Died There

Q. What additional Native Americans came under United States jurisdiction in 1867?

A. The Inuit and Aleut of Alaska, which was bought from Russia for $7.2 million.

Q. Aside from the bison, perhaps the most prized animal west of the Mississippi was the beaver. Some tribes even ascribed virtually human abilities to the animal, perhaps because of its cooperative dam-building society. Did Native Americans therefore refuse to hunt beaver?

A. Not all. As with the bison, the beaver was held in great respect, and there were many rituals that paid homage to it, but most tribes had no reluctance to skin it for its highly useful fur or, in some cases, to eat its flesh. Like all other creatures, the beaver was seen as part of a greater whole, in which it played its part and the Native American tribes played their part.

Q. What was the purpose of the Railroad Enabling Act of 1866?

131

A. It allowed the seizure of still more Native American lands for railroad rights-of-way. And the railroads would of course bring a further wave of settlers. Every step taken in the name of national progress across the West inevitably led to the dissolution of the Native American way of life.

Q. The Chisholm Trail, from Texas through Native American territory into Kansas, was marked out in 1866 by a fur trader named Jesse Chisholm, who drove a heavily loaded wagon of buffalo hides across the prairie, moving north from Texas to his trading post in Kansas. The heaviness of the wagon left ruts deep enough to be followed by other travelers. The route became the most favored for driving Texas longhorns north to the railhead depot lines that sprang up across Kansas, from Abilene to Ellsworth to Dodge City. Jesse Chisholm was part Native American. Was he part Choctaw, part Osage, or part Cherokee?

A. A strikingly handsome man, he was part Cherokee.

Q. Since the Chisholm Trail passed through Native American Territory, were the cattle drovers in particular danger of attack?

132

Something Else Died There

A. There were occasional incidents, but for the most part the Native Americans of various tribes simply charged a toll, usually ten cents a head, for the right to drive the herd across their lands.

Q. While Red Cloud's war was being waged in the Powder River country, there were also serious problems in Kansas. General Winfield Scott Hancock, the hero of Gettysburg who was later the Democratic nominee for President in 1880, was sent to try to bring the situation under control. Was he a good choice for this task?

A. No. He was a brilliant tactician, and immensely brave, but he had a contempt for Native Americans that bordered on loathing. The government wanted all Native Americans in this area of the plains to live south of the Arkansas River, and many had already moved there. But there were numerous chiefs determined to hang on to their bison hunting grounds rather than be relegated to the south to raise cattle. Hancock had been dispatched to stop a full-scale war from occurring, but with a series of high-handed actions, including the burning of Native American villages, he had further inflamed the situation.

Q. Hancock was recalled, and General Sherman was sent in his place. Was he successful?

A. To a large extent, he was, and at Medicine Lodge in October 1867 he got many of the most important chiefs to sign a treaty by which they agreed to stay below the Arkansas. Perhaps the most important chief of the southern Cheyenne, Sauts, whose name meant "bat" but whom whites called Roman Nose, refused to sign.

Q. Roman Nose was famous not only among his own people but also among the general public because he claimed to have a magic headdress that made him invincible, and so it seemed to many. He continued to cause trouble for another eleven months. But as he prepared to go into battle in September 1868, he knew that he would die that day. Is it true or false that his foreknowledge of death had to do with something that he had eaten?

A. It is true. A few days earlier, while visiting the Sioux, he had unwittingly eaten fried bread that had been cooked at the end of an iron fork. He believed that for iron to touch his food was destructive to his magic, and he immediately underwent purification rituals when he discovered what he had eaten. The battle, however, came too soon, before he could complete the rituals. And he was indeed killed that day.

Q. Name the major Civil War general who said, "The only good Indians I ever saw were dead."

Something Else Died There

A. General Philip H. Sheridan, who had even less use for Native Americans than he had had for Confederates. The occasion for his famous statement came in 1868, when as commander of the U.S. forces on the central plains, he received the surrender of a Comanche named Tosawi, who pointed to himself and said, "Tosawi, good Indian." Sheridan did not in fact have the implacable hatred of Native Americans that had marked one of his predecessors, General Winfield Scott Hancock, but he did regard them as "savages" and was determined to see the last of them bottled up on reservations.

Q. The Fourteenth Amendment to the Constitution, ratified in 1868, is most famous for its guarantee of due process or equal protection under the law. But it has other aspects. What did one of these do to Native Americans?

A. The amendment also defines citizenship and specifically states that Native Americans do not have the right to vote. The usurpation of the North American continent from its native peoples was now complete.

Q. How long did it take before the Native American right to vote became fully protected?

135

A Hahe, a Wichita, was known as the the Indian Madonna.

Something Else Died There

A. The right to vote was gradually restored in many states, but others resisted, and it was not until nearly one hundred years later that the 1965 Voting Rights Act gave full protection to all minorities, including Native Americans.

Q. In 1869 Native Americans were surprised to hear that the new President, Ulysses S. Grant, had appointed a full-blooded Seneca to be commissioner of Indian affairs. He was called Ely Samuel Parker, but his Seneca name was Donehogawa, which meant "Keeper of the Western Door of the Long House of the Iroquois." As a child, Parker had on his own initiative enrolled in a missionary school because he was tired of being teased by the officers at the Army post where he worked as a stableboy for not being able to speak English well. Thwarted in an attempt to become a lawyer, he studied civil engineering at Rensselaer Polytechnic Institute, worked on the Erie Canal, and was then hired by the federal government as a construction supervisor on various projects. In 1860 he met and became friendly with Grant in Galena, Illinois. What was Grant doing at the time?

A. A former Army captain, Grant was a clerk in a harness shop. Parker, of course, later became Grant's military secretary during the Civil War.

Q. Congress passed legislation in 1871 that ended what kind of negotiation with Native Americans?

A. The negotiation of treaties. From that time either acts of Congress or executive orders would be used to govern Native American affairs.

Q. During the two decades following 1870 what drug came into increasing use in religious ceremonies among North American Native Americans?

A. Peyote, dried cactus that helps induce visions, spread from the Native Americans of Mexico to such North American tribes as the Comanche and the Kiowa.

Q. In the early 1870s numerous tribal burial grounds were pillaged by whites, who disinterred and removed the bones. What did they do with the bones?

A. Sold them to be used in making buttons.

Q. Treaties protecting Native American lands in the Black Hills of South Dakota were widely broken beginning in 1874. What was the cause?

Something Else Died There

A. Gold had been discovered there.

Q. What were Dog Soldiers?

a. U.S. infantry
b. the Inuit name for sled-pulling huskies
c. a military society of the Cheyenne

A. The answer is c. Among the Plains Indians in particular, specialized societies of warriors played an integral part in the structure of the tribes. There were numerous such societies—one might almost call them fraternities—but the Dog Soldiers of the Cheyenne were especially noteworthy. In battle one of a party of ten would ride ahead and, after dismounting, drive his lance through a black sash tied around his neck. He would remain on the ground as the battle progressed, cheering on his fellow society members. Unless his comrades were victorious or came to a unanimous decision to retreat and removed the lance from his scarf, the grounded warrior was often killed where he was pinioned.

The slang term "dogface," used to refer to infantry in World War I, may be derived from the Dog Soldiers of the Cheyenne.

Q. The Modoc of northern California, a fairly small tribe, signed a treaty in 1864 by which they ceded their lands and agreed to live on the Oregon reservation of the more populous Klamath. But a young Modoc named Kintpuash— called Captain Jack by whites—did not like life on the reservation or being pushed around by the Klamath and led about sixty warriors and their families back to their old home ground on the Lost River, just over the California border. How swift was government retaliation for this action?

A. The government ignored it for several years, but as more and more whites moved into the area, with its lakes and lava plateaus, pressure was brought to oust the Modoc. The U.S. cavalry attacked Captain Jack's village on November 29, 1872, after all efforts at persuasion had failed. Captain Jack and some of his people retreated across Tule Lake in boats, while another leader called Hooker Jim rode around the lake, killing settlers as he went.

Q. Captain Jack and Hooker Jim rejoined forces in an area of lava rock that provided a natural fortress. For four months the sixty-odd Modoc warriors held off a large force of Regular Army and volunteer soldiers. How many men were finally ranged against the Modoc?

    a. 400
    b. 700
    c. 1,000

Something Else Died There

A. The answer is c. But even though Captain Jack's position was virtually impregnable, he realized that he would eventually run out of ammunition, so when a peace party arrived, he decided to negotiate.

Q. Hooker Jim derided Captain Jack for negotiating, and the majority were with him. What fatal step did Hooker Jim and a medicine man named Curly Headed Doctor persuade Jack to take?

A. To kill the members of the peace commission. On April 11, 1873—which happened to be Good Friday—Jack and two attendant warriors suddenly drew guns. Jack killed the head of the commission, General Edward R. S. Canby; another warrior killed the Reverend Eleasar Thomas; and a third commissioner was badly wounded. There had been some public sympathy for Captain Jack, but it was now replaced by outrage. Fresh forces were brought in, the Medoc were split into smaller bands—partially because of continued disagreements among themselves—and Captain Jack was finally captured on June 1, tried for murdering settlers, and hanged. It had actually been Hooker Jim who had murdered the settlers, but he testified against Captain Jack and was subsequently sent to a reservation.

Q. In 1874 raids by Native Americans in Texas on white buffalo hunters—who took only skins and left carcasses by the thousands—caused the military to clamp down. Large numbers of Native Americans left the reservations as a result, since they were being classified as "hostile," and soon nearly five thousand Comanche, Cheyenne, and Kiowa were gathered in the Panhandle, particularly around the forks of the Red River. Soldiers poured into the area, and the ensuing conflict came to be called the Red River War. Were there many major battles in this war?

A. No. There were so many soldiers that they were largely able to harass the Native Americans into eventual capitulation. A tremendously hot summer, sodden fall, and cold winter wore the tribespeople down, and the war was all over by the spring of 1875.

Q. Only three women have had their portraits appear on U.S. currency. Martha Washington was on the face of both the 1886 and the 1891 silver certificates, and Susan B. Anthony on the shunned 1979 one-dollar coin. Who was the third woman?

A. Pocahontas, who appeared on the back of the 1875 twenty-dollar bill. This undoubtedly reflected the so-called peace policy of

142

Something Else Died There

President Grant, which was in tatters by the end of his second term, following conflicts in many parts of the plains and the West.

Q. What was Greasy Grass, and where was it?

A. It was a vast meadowland on the banks of the Little Bighorn River in Montana. There, in late June 1876, some three thousand warriors under the leadership of Sitting Bull were encamped. This combined force of Sioux and Cheyenne had been stirring up endless trouble, but largely in separate areas. The U.S. Army under the overall command of General Sheridan had no idea that these various tribal units had massed together on the Greasy Grass.

Q. A few weeks earlier, during the annual Sun Dance, Sitting Bull had had a vision of dying soldiers. In which of the following ways did he describe these soldiers?

a. "an army of ghosts"
b. "falling right into our camp"
c. "cowards on the run"

A. The answer is b. Indeed, that is exactly what General George Armstrong Custer and his 264 men did on Sunday, June

24. They were slaughtered to the last man. But this great Native American victory soon backfired. The entire country was outraged, political settlements with the Native Americans fell into almost total disrepute, and much larger forces were marshaled against the tribes. The Battle of the Little Bighorn became a classic example of the Pyrrhic victory.

Q. The new influx of soldiers soon had Sitting Bull, Crazy Horse, and other chiefs on the run. In the spring of 1877 Sitting Bull decided that it was impossible to live together in the Black Hills with whites, and he would not go to a reservation, so he decided to lead his people to Grandmother's land. What was Grandmother's land?

A. Canada, ruled by Queen Victoria, whom the Native Americans called Grandmother.

Q. Did the people of Canada welcome Sitting Bull and his people?

A. They did not try to drive them away, but the Canadian Parliament was wary and assigned additional Mounties to keep track

Something Else Died There

of him. Aid of any kind was refused, and the American Sioux suffered greatly through the long winters. Sitting Bull's entreaties that a reservation be set aside for his people were ignored. Finally, on July 19, 1881, Sitting Bull returned to North Dakota and, along with 186 surviving tribespeople, surrendered at Fort Buford. Sitting Bull was killed by the Indian Police on December 15, 1890, supposedly while resisting arrest.

Q. The Nez Percé Indians of Washington State, who had befriended Lewis and Clark, had been at peace with whites for the intervening half century when in 1855 they were asked to sign a new treaty. It left them with ten thousand square miles in their ancestral Wallowa Valley, bisected by the Walla Walla River and bounded on the north and east by the Snake River. Aware of what was happening elsewhere, they agreed, but the Christianized old Chief Joseph was so embittered that he tore up his Bible. How many years did this treaty last?

A. Until 1863, when the increase in white settlers brought a demand that they give up all but one thousand square miles in western Idaho. The Nez Percé stayed where they were, however. Old Chief Joseph died in 1871, and his sons Joseph, who had attended a missionary school and was about thirty, and Ollikut, became the leaders.

Geronimo's other famous photograph, this portrait was
taken near the end of his life. He died in 1909.

Something Else Died There

Q. With increased pressure to relocate to Idaho, Joseph petitioned President Grant to let them remain where they were, according to the 1855 treaty. Did Grant agree?

A. Yes, but political pressure and a campaign of lies about the Nez Percé caused him to reverse his stand only two years later.

Q. General Oliver O. Howard was ordered in 1877 to remove the Nez Percé to Idaho. Howard thought this was wrong but was determined to carry out the order anyway. Why?

A. Because his reputation had never recovered from the fair treatment he had given Cochise four years earlier (he had sided with Cochise in a land dispute against white settlers).

Q. A series of incidents quickly led to confrontation and a battle that Joseph and Ollikut lost at White Bird Creek to the east of the Snake River on June 17. But most of the Nez Percé survived and were able to escape. With about 150 warriors and 550 women, children, and old men, the tribe then began a dodging trek through the territories of Idaho,

Wyoming, and Montana toward the Canadian border and a hoped-for haven with Sitting Bull. The desperate journey lasted three and a half months. How many miles did it cover?

    a. 1,200
    b. 1,700
    c. 2,000

A. The answer is b. Joseph and Ollikut and the chiefs Looking Glass and White Bird managed to outwit and outfight General Howard's forces at every turn. But their losses were heavy, too, and by the end of September only Joseph and White Bird were left as chiefs as they camped thirty miles south of Canada.

Q. Joseph and White Bird were soon ringed by soldiers. Surrender seemed the only option. White Bird and his followers managed to escape through the lines, but Joseph remained, surrendering for his remaining four hundred people, only eighty of them men. As he surrendered, did Chief Joseph have anything much to say?

A. Yes, he made one of the most famous speeches of all Native American chiefs, which was translated and taken down as he spoke.

148

Something Else Died There

He spoke of the deaths of the other chiefs and concluded with these sentences: "It is cold and we have no blankets. The little children are freezing to death. My people, some of them, have run away to the hills, and have no blankets, no food, no one knows where they are—perhaps freezing to death. I want to have time to look for my children and see how many I can find. Maybe I shall find them among the dead. Hear me, my chiefs. I am tired; my heart is sick and sad. From where the sun now stands I will fight no more forever."

Q. Did Chief Joseph and General Howard ever meet again?

A. Yes, the old enemies met in 1904 and posed for a photograph together. General Howard looks very distinguished and somber. Chief Joseph looks deeply sad. The chief died later that year, and the reservation doctor stated, "Joseph died of a broken heart."

Q. It is often written that many of the tribes of the Northwest Coast kept slaves—usually captured members of other tribes. Were these slaves of the same kind as the African Americans who fueled the economy of the pre–Civil War South?

A. No. While they did many menial jobs, they did not actually play a large enough part in the economics of the tribe even to cover the expense of keeping them. Instead they were status symbols: If a man was wealthy enough to have slaves, he was certainly important. Many historians and anthropologists object to calling them slaves at all and refer to them instead as captives.

Q. The U.S. Congress appropriated money in 1878 for the creation of an Indian Police. To what courts did these police report?

A. Initially to state courts, but in 1883 an Indian Court of Offenses was created. Another act, in 1885, formally gave the federal court system jurisdiction over major crimes committed by Native Americans.

Q. The fact that hogs were digging up and eating what whites called the wild hyacinths on the Camas Prairie of Idaho caused a war to break out in 1878. Is this true or false?

A. This is true. The camas root, a member of the hyacinth family, was one of the principal foods of several major tribes, includ-

Something Else Died There

ing the Shoshone, the Bannock, and the Flathead. By treaty, they had the right to dig for the roots on the Camas Prairie, but the hogs raised by the increasing numbers of white settlers decided that this was a delicacy particularly to their taste. The Bannock War ensued, but the Native Americans were defeated at Birch Creek on July 8.

Q. In the early 1880s many private organizations came into being that had what purpose in respect to Native Americans?

A. Organizations such as the Indian Protection Committee and the National Indian Defense Association were founded to aid Native Americans in a variety of ways. There had long been individuals who had decried the treatment of Native Americans, but these new organizations were testimony to a wider public awareness—and sense of shame—concerning the destruction of the Native American way of life.

Q. In 1876 settlers in Nebraska were alarmed to see a group of thirty-odd warriors, led by the Ponca chief Standing Bear, crossing territory that was supposedly cleared of Native Americans who had been relocated to Indian Territory to the south by an act of Congress. The authorities were notified, and the U.S. cavalry arrested Standing Bear and his followers. When the purpose of his journey became known, however, there was an upsurge of sympathy among the whites in Omaha, where the Ponca chief had been imprisoned. Why was Standing Bear in Nebraska Territory?

A. Standing Bear's son had just died, and his daughter had died recently. The Ponca chief wanted to bury his children in their ancestral lands. This was not a party of Indians on the warpath but a funeral procession. Two white lawyers took Standing Bear's case, requesting the U.S. district court to issue a writ of habeas corpus, freeing Standing Bear. Federal prosecutors claimed that because Indians were not defined as persons in the Constitution, habeas corpus did not apply. The judge who heard the case, Elmer S. Dundy, ruled in favor of Standing Bear, and a new legal precedent was set. Standing Bear was allowed to continue his journey and to bury his children.

Q. One of the most famous chiefs of the Chiricahua Apache was named Goyathlay, meaning "One Who Yawns," but he was given a different name, by which he is remembered, that was based on the Spanish name for Saint Jerome. What name do we know him by?

Sacheen Littlefeather, dressed in Apache dress, was selected by Marlon
Brando to accept the Academy Award for Best Actor he won for his
role in *The Godfather*. Brando would not accept himself "because of
the treatment of the American Indian in motion pictures and tele-
vision and because of recent happenings at Wounded Knee."

A. Geronimo.

Q. Geronimo was the preeminent leader in a series of Apache raids and uprisings in New Mexico and Arizona from 1881 to 1886. He was much feared by the whites in the area but bordered on being a hero to schoolboys in the East. What was it about Geronimo's exploits that so appealed to schoolboys?

A. Whenever he was put in an untenable situation, Geronimo surrendered. But then he would put together a party of warriors and go on the warpath again. In 1886, having surrendered for the third time, Geronimo escaped with several warriors even as they were being escorted back to a reservation by a sizable military force. This particular escapade was so embarrassing that the commanding general, the famous Indian fighter General George Crook, was replaced. Eight months later, however, Geronimo was captured again, and he and his more than three hundred warriors were sent to Florida as prisoners of war; some of these warriors had served as scouts for the U.S. Army in the past. After four years at hard labor, he was sent to Fort Sill in Oklahoma, where he became a Christian and died at the age of seventy-five in 1909.

Q. In 1888 a young Paiute in Nevada, Wovoka, the son of a shaman, fell ill. While he was consumed by fever, there was an eclipse of the sun. He then proclaimed that he had had a vision announcing the imminent appearance of a Native American messiah. He prophesied that the world would end, but then all Native Americans, those living at the time as well as their ancestors, would be reborn and would henceforth live in harmony. What was the name given to the new religion that this vision inspired?

A. *The Ghost Dance. Although Wovoka never traveled from his home area near Walker Lake, Paiute disciples spread the world, and many chiefs and medicine men came to see him. The Ghost Dance took hold with great speed, spreading widely, and by 1890 it had become a virtual craze among the dejected Plains Indians. Sitting Bull became its leading advocate but gave the prophecy a new spin by promoting the idea that the coming apocalypse would also eradicate the white man.*

Q. Virtually alone among the major tribes, the Navajo completely rejected the Ghost Dance. Why?

A. *Their religion fostered a great fear of the dead and of ghosts, and the very idea of their ancestors rising from the grave terrified them.*

Q. White authorities were extremely disturbed by the speed with which the Ghost Dance spread and the fervor with which it was adopted. Fearing another rebellion, soldiers under General Nelson Miles were dispatched to South Dakota. This only made the situation more volatile, and two chiefs, Kicking Bear and Short Bull, tried to gather a force in the northwestern corner of South Dakota's Pine Ridge Reservation in December 1890. They sent a message to Sitting Bull to join them. Did he do so?

A. No, he was arrested by the Indian Police and killed while supposedly "resisting arrest."

Q. Big Foot, a chief of the Miniconjou, did head for Pine Ridge. General Miles sent out the Seventh Cavalry to prevent his approach. Why was this a mistake?

A. Big Foot was not coming to join the rebellious Kicking Bear. He had been summoned by the seventy-two-year-old Red Cloud, who favored the idea of the military's restoring order. Because of one misunderstanding after another, fueled by decades of mistrust, the outcome was a massacre of Big Foot and his people at Wounded Knee on December 29. It was somewhere near Wounded Knee

Something Else Died There

Creek that the parents of Crazy Horse had buried their son's bones and heart thirteen years earlier in 1877. The 1890 massacre at Wounded Knee sounded a final knell for the Native American hope of restoring their way of life. The promise of the Ghost Dance was unfulfilled.

The Sioux holy man Black Elk summed up what had happened:

I did not know then how much was ended. When I look back now from this high hill of my old age, I can still see the butchered women and children lying heaped and scattered all along the crooked gulch as plain as I saw them with eyes still young. And I can see that something else died there in the bloody mud, and was buried there in the blizzard. A people's dream died there. It was a beautiful dream.

And I, to whom so great a vision was given in my youth—you see me now a pitiful old man who has done nothing, for the nation's hoop is broken and scattered. There is no center any longer, and the sacred tree is dead.

Chapter Five: *New Beginnings?*

Q. The General Allotment Act, passed in 1887, began to have a profound effect on Native Americans in the 1890s. Under the act the reservations were to be divided into 160-acre parcels, with a parcel to be awarded to the head of each family. Supposedly this was done to encourage Native American self-sufficiency. But what was the real effect?

A. It destroyed tribal authority. The hidden agenda of the Congress was to "Americanize" the remaining Native Americans.

Q. Was there any significant resistance to the Allotment Act by Native American tribes?

A. Yes, both the Cherokee and the Choctaw rejected the idea and tried to fight it in court. Congress's answer was the Curtis Act of 1898, which brought the hidden agenda into the open by ending tribal government and imposing allotment on the two tribes.

Q. Were whites able to get their hands on more Native American lands as the result of the allotment policy?

A. Yes. Initially, after tribal lands had been allotted to the heads of families, any surplus could be given to non–Native Americans. Since not all the land allotted to Native Americans was actually farmed, new legislation made it possible for the Native American owners to lease land to whites. But corrupt officials and underhanded deals led to much land being bought outright by whites for far less than its value. In addition, as soon as a Native American family began to make a profit on farming its land, they were hit by the heavy taxes levied by many states, and many Native Americans lost their lands as a result.

Q. In 1899 Major J. W. Powell, who was sympathetic to the plight of Native Americans, suggested a new word to use instead of "Indian." What was it?

A. "Amerind." But it never really took hold among either whites or Native Americans, although a Native American organization founded in the 1960s calls itself AMERIND.

Q. What kinds of leases on Native American lands were first made to white-owned companies in 1902?

New Beginnings?

A. Oil and gas leases were made by the secretary of the interior on land in Oklahoma.

Q. One of the reasons President Theodore Roosevelt is still held in high regard today is that he was the first President to be an ardent conservationist. Why do many Native Americans have very mixed feelings about his policies in this area?

A. Under Roosevelt the federal government developed a habit of seizing Native American lands to turn into national parks. For example, in 1906, 50,000 acres of land sacred to the Taos Pueblo Indians were seized in New Mexico, and only five days before the end of his second term in 1909, Roosevelt signed executive orders that turned 2.5 million acres of Native American land across the country into national forests.

Q. In 1910 the federal government created a full-scale medical service for Native Americans. This was certainly welcome, but that same year the government also banned one of the most important Native American rituals, supposedly on "medical" grounds. What was this ritual?

A. The Sun Dance of the Plains Indians. The authorities cited the prevalence of self-torture during the dance as the reason for banning it.

Q. The U.S. Mint issued the famous Buffalo Head nickel in 1913. Chiefs of which three tribes were used in the composite portrait on the reverse side from the buffalo?

A. Chiefs of the Cheyenne, the Seneca, and the Sioux.

Q. Why was Jim Thorpe, who was part Sauk, forced to return the decathlon and pentathlon medals he had won in 1912 at the Olympic Games in Stockholm?

A. It was discovered that he had briefly played semipro baseball. Thorpe, a product of the famous Carlisle Indian School, nevertheless entered into legend as perhaps the greatest male athlete of all time in the United States. His medals were restored posthumously in 1983.

Q. In terms of census figures, something happened for the first time in fifty years among Native Americans in 1917. What was it?

New Beginnings?

A. There were more births than deaths among the Native American tribes. During the previous twenty-five years the Native American population had been at an all-time low, hovering below 250,000. But after 1917 it began to grow once more.

Q. What new Native American institution was incorporated in Oklahoma in 1918, under the sponsorship of several tribes?

A. The Native American Church. The original tribes involved were Kiowa, Comanche, Apache, and Cheyenne, but within a dozen years about half the Native Americans in the country had joined this church. Its rituals made use of peyote, the dried cactus that produces color hallucinations. The U.S. government has always regarded this use of peyote with a jaundiced eye, but since there is no evidence that it is habit-forming, and thus cannot be classified as a narcotic, attempts over the years to ban its use have been fruitless.

Q. Did any Native Americans fight in World War I?

A. Yes, they enlisted in considerable numbers. It was partially as recognition of their contributions that the Citizenship Act was passed in 1924, making all Native Americans citizens of the land they had once ruled.

Q. Did citizenship automatically bring with it the right to vote?

A. No. Most states granted it, but not until 1948 did Arizona recognize this right. Maine did so in 1954, but New Mexico didn't until 1962. All three states were forced to grant the right to vote by court decree or federal intervention.

Q. Senator Charles Curtis of Kansas was elected Vice President of the United States as Herbert Hoover's running mate in 1928. Did he have a good record in respect to Native American affairs?

A. Yes, excellent. Part Kaw, he remains the highest elected official of Native American ancestry in U.S. history.

Q. A Senate committee investigating Native American affairs in 1930 uncovered evidence that in their zeal to educate

New Beginnings?

Navajo children, Bureau of Indian Affairs officials had sanctioned what sort of activity?

A. The kidnapping of Navajo children from their parents.

Q. A number of private and public commissions began to attack the thirty-year-old allotment policy in the 1920s. By the time Franklin D. Roosevelt was elected in 1932, a fresh approach was clearly in order. Roosevelt chose a man named John Collier to become commissioner of Indian affairs. Was this appointment welcomed by Native Americans?

A. It was a cause for rejoicing: In 1923 Collier had founded the American Indian Defense Association. There had been many organizations devoted to Native American welfare in the late nineteenth century, but almost all had fallen by the wayside, seemingly redundant in the wake of allotment policy.

Q. The Indian Reorganization Act of 1934 abolished the practice of allotment. Did it also restore tribal government?

A. Yes, tribal self-government was now encouraged.

Q. What provisions were made to deal with tribes whose lands had been allotted to others and who were therefore essentially without a homeland?

A. The Oklahoma Indian Welfare Act was passed in 1936 to deal with this problem.

Q. Aside from these economic and political matters, was any step taken to recognize the uniqueness of Native American cultural life?

A. Yes, Congress created the Indian Arts and Crafts Board also in 1934, to foster and preserve Native American art.

Q. Native Americans of Iroquois descent, particularly Mohawk, have long been regarded as among the best high steelworkers there are and have had a part in the construction of most of the major suspension bridges and skyscrapers in America. Is this just an accident of history or are there cultural reasons for it?

A. The tribes of the Iroquois League have a history of being at ease when working at heights that goes back well beyond the first

New Beginnings?

European contacts with them. They used tree bark as a building material and, in order to procure long sheets of it, would climb high up to make an incision down the length of the trunk. The high steelworking tradition started in 1886, when a cantilever bridge was under construction across the St. Lawrence Seaway. One end of the bridge was anchored in Native American–held land, and in recompense the Mohawk demanded jobs in the building of the bridge. They were given very lowly postions at first but soon proved themselves tremendously adept at riveting together steel beams at high altitudes. More and more Mohawk, who found the risks inherent in high steelwork a psychologically satisfying substitute for the ancient trials of warriors, took up the profession. By the late 1940s a ten-square-block community in the North Gowanus section of Brooklyn had become an almost entirely Mohawk high steelworker enclave.

Q. During the Second World War how many Native Americans served in the military?

   a. 15,000
   b. 25,000
   c. 30,000

A. The answer is b.

Q. What special code did marines of Navajo ancestry use during battles that completely flummoxed the enemy?

A. Their own language. A Navajo alphabet had been introduced in the years just prior to the war.

Q. During the 1940s and 1950s two Osage sisters became world-famous ballerinas. Can you name them?

A. Maria Tallchief rose to fame with the Ballet Russe de Monte Carlo and then became one of the great stars of George Balanchine's New York City Ballet. Her younger sister, Marjorie Tallchief, became a prima ballerina of the Paris Opéra Ballet and was particularly famous for her incandescent dancing in Igor Stravinsky's Rite of Spring.

Q. In the years immediately following World War II, still another change in government policy toward Native Americans began to take shape. Was the emerging policy a step forward or backward in terms of Native American self-government?

New Beginnings?

A. It was, of course, painted by the federal government as a step forward, but in reality its effect would be to undermine tribal units. Washington once again was determined to push Native Americans toward a greater degree of assimilation and encourage movement away from reservations and into urban settings. The policy was officially put forward in the Termination Resolution of 1953, which called for an end to the "trusteeship" of reservations by the federal government. Initially it was to affect only certain tribes in some states, but it was seen as a long-term effort to "help" the Native American tribes join the great "melting pot" of American society.

Q. Did the start of the cold war and the inflammatory anti-Communist rhetoric of the McCarthyite era have anything to do with the formulation of the termination policy?

A. It had a great deal to do with it. In the hysteria of the times, which can seem darkly comic in retrospect, there were many anti-Communist zealots who were extremely worried about the fact that Native American tribes had a communal culture. This way of life, which Native Americans had practiced for several thousand years, was suddenly viewed as having a philosophical connection to communism. Visions of Communist cells forming among tribes had many politicians in a lather, and their answer to this wholly imaginary threat was to try to hustle Native Americans off to the cities to become urban cogs in the capitalist machine.

Q. How long did Washington's termination fever last?

A. It was at its height for only about eight years, and the termination policy began to be reversed in 1961. But by that time more than sixty tribes and other Native American communities had lost both the services and protections of the federal government. It was a disaster from which numerous tribes are still trying to recover.

Q. What kind of reaction did the termination policy create among Native Americans?

A. At first there was little outcry; especially to older Native Americans, this was just one more betrayal in an endless procession that stretched back to the seventeenth century. But by the early 1960s younger Indians began to marshal themselves to gain better control of their destiny. The National Indian Youth Conference held in New Mexico in 1961 was one of many signs that a new generation

New Beginnings?

of Native Americans was prepared to take a much stronger position in the years to come.

Q. Under the administration of John F. Kennedy, the repressive attitude toward Native Americans that had existed in the Eisenhower years began to change. Was this just a matter of reversing the termination policy, or was a new look at the lot of Native Americans taken across the board?

A. There was a real change. In 1961 alone three commissions set up by the Kennedy administration issued reports: the Keeler Commission on Indian Affairs, the Brophy Commission on Rights, Liberties and Responsibilities of the American Indian, and the United States Commission on Civil Rights. All three advocated different kinds of programs that would bolster the self-determination and economic potential of Native Americans.

Q. What was to become the most famous—some would say notorious—Native American pressure group was founded in 1968 in Minneapolis. Name it.

A. The American Indian Movement, commonly called AIM, led by Russell Means and Dennis Banks.

Q. In 1968 President Lyndon Johnson delivered a special message to Congress, calling for a National Council on Indian Opportunity. What phrase did he use to describe the Native American population?

A. His message was titled "The Forgotten American."

Q. The Resolution of the Thirty Tribes was drawn up by Native American activists in 1968. What was it intended to thwart?

A. A bill making its way through Congress called the Indian Resources Development Act, which was supposed to give the final say on all Native American land dealing to the Department of the Interior. The resolution, in combination with other lobbying efforts, succeeded in derailing the legislation.

Q. The same year saw the founding of what kind of institution on a reservation?

A. The Navajo Community College was the first four-year college ever to exist on a reservation. It served as another step in the direction of Native American self-determination.

174

New Beginnings?

Q. The site of what former maximum security prison was seized by Native Americans in 1969?

A. *Alcatraz, the island in San Francisco Bay, was held by Native Americans until 1971 and then in 1972 became a part of the Golden Gate National Recreation Area. The reason the Native Americans had occupied it was that it was unused, thus "surplus," federal land that the Native Americans had a right to reclaim under the law, although the federal government did not see it that way.*

Q. What was the special significance of the novel *House Made of Dawn*?

A. *Its author, N. (Navarre) Scott Momaday, born on the Kiowa reservation in Oklahoma, became the first Native American to win the Pulitzer Prize for literature with this novel in 1969. Among his other notable books are the collection of Kiowa folktales* The Way to Rainy Mountain, *the book of poems* The Gourd Dancer, *and* The Names: A Memoir.

Q. The Blue Lake Wilderness Area of New Mexico, land that had been the ancestral home of the Taos Pueblo, had been seized by the federal government in 1906 and made a part of the National Park system. What happened to the land in 1970?

A. It was finally returned to the Taos people, to whom it was sacred.

Q. Spearheaded by AIM, but with the participation of seven other Native American groups, a march on Washington, called the Trail of the Broken Treaties March, was organized for a major date on the federal calendar in 1972. What date was it?

A. Election day, November 4. When officials, from President Nixon on down, failed to meet with the Native American leaders, they took over the Bureau of Indian Affairs for five days, and in their attempts to barricade themselves against riot squads, they did considerable damage.

Q. When an Oglala Sioux from Pine Ridge was beaten and then paraded around naked from the waist down in Gordon, Nebraska, in February 1972, it was at first just another

New Beginnings?

example of the vigilante violence against Native Americans by whites in Gordon. But when he was found dead a week later, his family tried unsuccessfully to get the authorities to charge the men involved in the beating. AIM leaders who were meeting in nearby Omaha drove to Gordon and led protests that eventually led to manslaughter convictions for two brothers by the name of Hare. Why was AIM's part in this event an important turning point?

A. Because the older, more traditional Native American leaders at Pine Ridge and other reservations had been wary about AIM, with its emphasis on urban Native American problems. All that now began to change, and AIM became increasingly involved in reservation problems.

Q. On the last day of February 1973 Native Americans, led by AIM founders Russell Means and Dennis Banks, took over the community of Wounded Knee on the Pine Ridge Reservation. Was this action caused primarily by government intransigence on Native American issues?

A. No. Although the government was dragging its feet on a wide variety of concerns, one of the problems was that the tribal

Chief Red Cloud in traditional portrait pose

178

New Beginnings?

leader, named Dick Wilson, was behaving in a despotic fashion and was clearly in the pocket of the government. One of the main demands of the protesters was for a change of tribal leaders.

Q. Aside from the AIM members, how many Oglala Sioux were involved in the occupation of Wounded Knee?

a. 100
b. 200
c. 325

A. The answer is b. The occupation quickly turned into a state of siege, as the FBI, the U.S. Marshal Service, and the Bureau of Indian Affairs police put together a small army and surrounded Wounded Knee.

Q. Despite attempts by Senators George McGovern and James Abourezk, who had long been sympathetic to Native Americans, to resolve the situation, the law enforcement units involved were determined to end the occupation without making any concessions. They were egged on by a considerable number of local bigots. Negotiations started periodically, but there were many exchanges of gunfire as well. When the exhausted remaining Native Americans finally gave up seventy-one days later, had any of their number been killed?

A. Yes, two. But it could have been far worse since there were many hotheads who wanted to launch a full-scale attack on the occupiers.

Q. Who was Sacheen Littlefeather, and at what televised event did she create a major stir in April 1973?

A. Sacheen Littlefeather was selected by Marlon Brando to appear in his stead at the Academy Awards ceremony that year if he were to win the Best Actor Oscar for The Godfather. *Dressed in an Apache costume, she caused a lot of comment even before the evening got under way. It was Brando's intention to refuse his Oscar to protest the treatment of American Indians, and Sacheen Littlefeather held a fifteen-page speech in her hand. But before the show she was warned by the producer of the telecast, Howard W. Koch, that he would have her "bodily removed" from the stage if she spoke for more than the forty-five seconds allotted to stand-ins for absent stars. When Brando did win, she gave a brief, dignified*

New Beginnings?

speech that was met with a mixture of applause and boos. Afterward the general conclusion of the Hollywood elite was that if Brando had wanted to refuse the Oscar in the name of Native American justice, he should at least have had the guts to do it himself.

Q. Even as both federal and state law enforcement officials continued to seek confrontations with Native American activists and to arrest Native Americans on any charges they could come up with, the U.S. Congress in 1975 passed an act that signaled the new attitudes toward Native Americans that were becoming more prevalent. There was a hyphenated word in the name of the act that said it all. What was that word?

A. Self-Determination. The Indian Self-Determination Act made it possible for tribes to take part in administering all federal programs affecting Native Americans. At long last the hope existed that Native Americans might have some real say in their own destiny.

Q. In 1975 there also took place a significant return of land to Native Americans. A total of 346,000 acres that had been in federal hands since 1933 was given back to Native

American control. How many tribes were affected by this action?

    a. eleven
    b. eighteen
    c. twenty-three

A. The answer is b. Eighteen tribes got some of their land back.

Q. Who is Leonard Peltier, and why is he controversial?

A. On June 26, 1975, at a shoot-out at the Pine Ridge Reservation in South Dakota, two FBI agents were killed. Peltier was tried and convicted of shooting them in 1977. But he has always denied his guilt, and the trial was marked by a large number of what many believe to be severe irregularities, including perjured testimony by Peltier's accusers. His case remains the subject of bitter debate, and there is an unending struggle to exonerate him.

Q. When the Indians Claims Commission, originally established in 1946, shut down in 1978, how much money had it paid to tribes in restitution for the seizure of their lands?

New Beginnings?

a. $200 million
b. $400 million
c. $800 million

A. The answer is c. About 60 percent of the claims were found valid. There were many cases, however, in which claims were dismissed for what amounted to technicalities.

Q. Under the Reagan and Bush administrations did funding for Native American programs increase or decrease?

A. It decreased by about 40 percent.

Q. In 1992 an apparent agreement was reached on a dispute in Arizona between two tribes over land. Which two tribes were involved?

A. The Hopi and the Navajo. The problem goes back to the nineteenth century, when arbitrary allotment of land by the federal government created artificial boundaries that did not conform to the actuality of the differing cultures of the sheepherding Navajo and the farming Hopi, an ironic echo of the range wars between white

cattlemen and farmers that are part of the legend of the "Old West."
Congress still has to approve the settlement, and there is every sign
that the deal will ultimately fall apart again. Some members of
Congress insist that public lands, legally owned by the federal
government, cannot be used to settle disputes between tribes. There
are still a great many people—powerful people—who cannot
grasp that the lands were stolen from Native Americans in the first
place.

Q. How many states have Native American names?

a. twenty-one
b. twenty-six
c. thirty-four

A. The answer is b. They are Alabama, Alaska, Arkansas,
Arizona, Connecticut, Idaho, Illinois, Iowa, Kansas, Kentucky,
Massachusetts, Michigan, Minnesota, Mississippi, Missouri, Ne-
braska, New Mexico, North Dakota, Ohio, Oklahoma, South
Dakota, Tennessee, Texas, Utah, Wisconsin, and Wyoming. It
should be noted that a number of Native American tribes were given
English names. Thus, although we speak of Delaware Indians,
"Delaware" is not a word drawn from a Native American language.
The Delaware were of Algonquian-Wakashan stock.

New Beginnings?

Q. Can you supply the missing word in the following statement of the renowned Chief Seattle? "The _____ is not his brother but his enemy, and when he has conquered it, he moves on."

A. The word is "earth," and Chief Seattle was talking about the white man's attitude toward land.

Q. "They had what the world has lost. What the world has lost, the world must have again, lest it die. . . . It is the lost reverence and passion for human personality, joined with the ancient lost reverence for the earth and the web of life." When were these words written?

    a. the 1890s
    b. the 1930s
    c. the 1980s

A. The answer is b. These words were written by President Franklin Delano Roosevelt's commissioner of Indian affairs. They hark back to a sense of loss and shame expressed by an enlightened few during the 1890s (and even earlier), while looking forward to the environmental concerns that would begin to develop seriously in the 1980s.

John Collier served as commissioner from 1934 to 1945 and probably did more than any single white man to reverse old strictures and offer new opportunities to Native Americans, but as his words suggest, a world had been lost, and much of it was irretrievable.

Bibliography

Bad Heart Bull, Amos, and Helen H. Blish. *A Pictographic History of the Oglala Sioux*. Lincoln: University of Nebraska Press, 1967.

Brandon, William. *Indians*. Boston: Houghton Mifflin, 1989.

Brown, Dee. *Bury My Heart at Wounded Knee*. New York: Bantam, 1973.

Catlin, George. *North American Indians*, 2 vol. New York: Dover Publications, 1973.

Ceram, C. W. *The First Americans*. New York: Harcourt, Brace, Jovanovich, 1971.

Collier, John. *Indians of the Americas*. New York: New American Library, 1975.

Bibliography

Cotterill, R. A. *The Southern Indians*. Norman: University of Oklahoma Press, 1954.

Cremony, John C. *Life Among the Apaches*. New York: Indian Head Books, 1991.

Deloria, Vine, Jr. *Behind the Trail of Broken Treaties*. New York: Delacorte, 1974.

De Vorsey, Louis, Jr. *The Indian Boundary in the Southern Colonies*. Chapel Hill: University of North Carolina Press, 1961.

Dorn, Edward, and Leroy Lucas. *The Shoshoneans*. New York: Morrow, 1966.

Drimmer, Frederick. *Captured by the Indians*. New York: Dover, 1961.

Driver, Harold E. *Indians of North America*. Chicago: University of Chicago Press, 1961.

Edmunds, R. David. *American Indian Leaders*. Lincoln: University of Nebraska Press, 1980.

Farb, Peter. *Man's Rise to Civilization*. New York: E. P. Dutton, 1968.

188

Bibliography

Goetzman, William E., and William N. Goetzman. *The West of the Imagination*. New York: Norton, 1986.

Grant, Bruce. *Concise Encylopedia of the American Indian*. New York: Bonanza Books, 1986.

Huddleston, Lee Eldridge. *Origins of the American Indian—European Concepts 1492–1729*. Austin: University of Texas, 1967.

Josephy, Alvin M., Jr. *The Indian Heritage of America*. New York: Knopf, 1968.

Limerick, Patricia Nelson. *The Legacy of Conquest*. New York: Norton, 1987.

Malone, John Williams. *An Album of the American Cowboy*. New York: Franklin Watts, 1971.

Martin, Paul S.; George I. Quimby; and Donald Collier. *Indians Before Columbus*. Chicago: University of Chicago Press, 1947.

Mathiessen, Peter. *In the Spirit of Crazy Horse*. New York: Viking, 1991.

Morison, Samuel Eliot. *The European Discovery of America*. New York: Oxford University Press, 1971.

Bibliography

Nabokov, Peter, ed. *Native American Testimony*. New York: Viking, 1991.

Neihardt, John G. *Black Elk Speaks*. Lincoln: University of Nebraska Press, 1961.

Oswalt, Wendell H. *This Land Was Theirs*. New York: John Wiley & Sons, 1973.

Poatgeiter, Hermia. *Indian Legacy*. New York: Julian Messner, 1981.

Silverberg, Robert. *Mound Builders of Ancient America*. Greenwich, Conn.: New York Graphic Society, 1968.

Stewart, George R. *American Place Names*. New York: Oxford University Press, 1970.

Swanton, John R. *The Indian Tribes of North America*. Washington, D.C.: Smithsonian Institution Press, 1974.

Utley, Robert M. *The Indian Frontier of the American West, 1846–1890*. Albuquerque: University of New Mexico Press, 1984.

Waldman, Carl. *Atlas of the North American Indian*. New York: Facts on File, 1985.

Warner, John Anson. *The Life and Art of the North American Indian*. Secaucus, N.J.: Chartwell Books, 1990.